WORLD LITERATURE 1-

SEM 2 MA ENGLISH(UNIVERSITY OF KERALA-2022 SYLLABUS)

PAPYRUS COLLECTION

Made with ♥ on the Notion Press Platform
www.notionpress.com

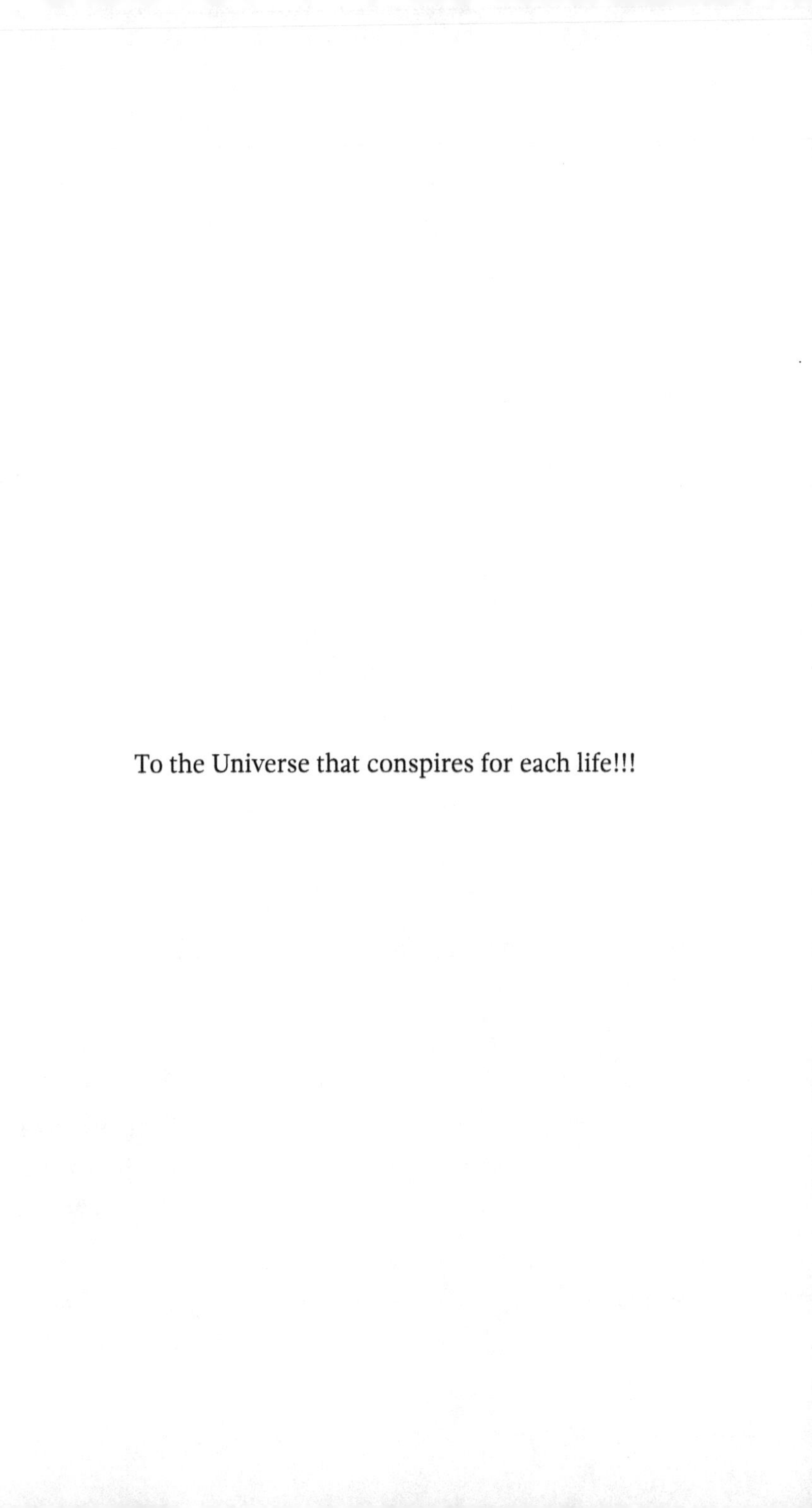

To the Universe that conspires for each life!!!

Contents

Contents

Foreword

Nothing begins and ends anywhere. the tree of knowledge supplants new ideas in you and me.
	Thank you

Preface

SEMESTER II
Paper V: EL.521 : X World Literatures I
(Core Course 5 :6 hours /week)

Aim: To read, understand and reflect on texts from different socio-cultural and historical
perspectives
Course Objectives
The objectives of this Course are to
• introduce students to world literature
• provide knowledge about cultural nationalism, multiculturalism and transnationalism in
the postcolonial world
• develop intellectual flexibility, inclusivity, creativity and cultural literacy
• contextualize the unique traditions of the world, including aspects of time and space
• critically discuss the subtleties involved in regional aesthetics
• familiarise students with the concepts of plurality in global voices
Course Outcome
The students would have
CO 1: Recognised the various socio-cultural and political experiences and expressions
seen in world literatures
CO 2: Learned the theoretical grounding to read literatures in English from different
regions
CO 3: Recognised the ways in which transcultural flows affect the readings of texts across

social and historical borders

CO 4: Analysed the discursive reach of English in shaping imaginative journeys across

continents

CO 5: gained an understanding through reading, discussion and writing about literatures

in different genre

Course Description

Module I : The Middle East

Module Outcome:

Students would have

MO 1: understood the socio-cultural background of Middle Eastern literature as well as place

space and borders as a method of critical inquiry.

MO 2: identified the poets, dramatist and novelist of the region

MO 3: acquired a theoretical grounding to read literatures in English from different region.

Unit -1

Dalya Cohen-Mor (Editor). "Arab women writers: A Brief Sketch".

(Arab Women Writers: An Anthology of Short Stories. New York State UP. 2005. Pp 3-7)

Al-Khansaa – "Sleepless I Kept the Night's Vigil" (poem)
https://www.poemhunter.com/poem/sleepless-i-kept-the-night-vigil/

Maram al Massi – (14) "Women Like Me..." (from A Red Cherry on a White Tiled Floor) (poem)

https://www.narrativemagazine.com/issues/poems-week-2008-2009/poem-week/red-cherry-white-tiled-floor-maram-al-massri

Tawfiq al-Hakim – The Sultan's Dilemma (play).

(from Denys Johnson-Davies (Editor). The Essential

Tawfiq Al-Hakim: Great Egyptian Writers
(Modern Arabic Literature). The American University in Cairo Press; Reprint edition, 2013.

Raja Alem – Dove's Necklace (novel) Abrams & Chronicle Books, Reprint edition, 2018.

Khaled Khalifa - Death is Hard Work (novel). Hachette – Antoine, 2016.

Module II: South Asia

Module Outcome:

Students will be able to

MO 1: understand the literatures of South Asia, the impact of colonialism, the trauma of partition
and its socio-political impacts in the area.

MO 2: Identify the poets, dramatist and novelist of the region

MO 3: understand the concepts of Post-colonialism, neo-colonialism, transculturation, power
dialogism, identity crisis, gender disparity and suppression.

Unit -2

Imtiaz Dharker – "Purdah I" (poem)
https://www.poetryinternational.org/pi/poem/2823/auto/0/0/Imtiaz-Dharker/PURDAH-1/en/tile

Tsering Wangmo Dhompa – "She Is" (poem)
https://www.poetryfoundation.org/poems/54718/she-is

Ko Ko Thett – "Political Science" (poem)
https://chajournal.blog/2021/03/09/ko-ko-thett/

Urvashi Butalia – "Honour" (from The Other Side of Silence: Voices from the Partition of India)
Penguin, 2007.

Mahmud Rahman – "Kerosene" (from Killing the Water) (short story). Penguin, 2010.

Mohammed Hanif – A Case of Exploding Mangoes (novel). Vintage Books, 2011.

Nayoni Munaweera – Island of a Thousand Mirrors (novel). St.Martins Press, 2014

Module III : Australia and New Zealand

Module Outcome:

Students would have

MO 1: understood the literatures of Australia and New Zealand, the aboriginal cultures and their

narratives

MO 2: learned about the impact of colonial settlements, the repression of the indigenous

population and their struggle for survival MO 3: evaluate the literary texts from a postcolonial

perspective

Unit - 3

Judith Wright – "Bullocky" (poem)

https://allpoetry.com/Bullocky

Banjo Paterson – "Waltzing Matilda" (poem)

https://allpoetry.com/Waltzing-Matilda

At the city pound by VIncent O'Sullivan (poem)

https://www.poetryfoundation.org/poetrymagazine/poems/145477/at-the-city-pound

Attitudes for a New Zealand Poet by Allen Curnow (poem)

https://www.poetryfoundation.org/poetrymagazine/browse?contentId=23694

Yellow Brick Road by Witi Ihimaera (Short Story)

https://englishwithhume.weebly.com/uploads/1/0/7/2/10723048/yellow_brick_road_by_witi_ihi

maera.pdf

David Malouf - Remembering Babylon (novel)

https://urpdf.net/remembering-babylon-pdf/

Patricia Grace - Potiki (novel). University of Hawaii Press, 1995.

Module IV: European, UK and Ireland

Module Outcome:

Students would have

MO 1: understood and identified key concepts in European Literature-Realism, Naturalism,

Expressionism, Symbolism, Surrealism etc

MO 2: learned about movements like Irish Literary Renaissance

MO 3: evaluated the social, political and cultural dimensions of the texts prescribed

Unit -4- European

Karin Boyes – Of Course It Hurts

https://www.karinboye.se/verk/dikter/dikter-engelska/of-course-it-hurts.shtml

Yehuda Amichai – Jews in the Land of Israel

https://www.poetryfoundation.org/poems/58629/jews-in-the-land-of-israel

Zofia Romanowics "To my little girl"

https://www.worldliteraturetoday.org/blog/poetry/four-poems-polish-holocaust-survivor-zofia-romanowicz

Fyodor Dostoyevsky – "The Heavenly Christmas Tree" (short story)

Italo Calvino – "Mushrooms in the City" from Marcovaldo (short story)

Wislawa Szymborska – "Utopia" (poem)

https://www.poemhunter.com/poem/utopia-27/

Unit -5- UK and Ireland

Philip Larkin - "Faith Healing"

https://www.poetryfoundation.org/poems/48413/faith-healing

Benjamin Zephania "People will always needeople"

https://www.best-poems.net/poem/people-will-always-need-people-by-benjamin-zephaniah.html

JM Synge – The Tinker's Wedding (play) https://www.gutenberg.org/files/1328/1328-h/1328-h.htm

Stephen Baxter – "Last Contact" (short story) https://epdf.tips/last-contact.html

Monica Ali – In the Kitchen (novel). Doubleday Publishers, 2009.

Reading List:

Boehmer, Elleke. Stories of Women: Gender and Narrative in the Postcolonial Nation.

Manchester UP. 2005.

Bondanella, Peter. "Italo Calvino and Umberto Eco: Postmodern Masters." The Cambridge

Companion to the Italian Novel. Ed. Peter Bondanella and Andrea Ciccarelli. Cambridge

UP. 2003. pp. 168 - 181.

Calder, Alex. The Writing of New Zealand: Inventions and Identities. Auckland UP.

2011.

Chomsky, Noam. "U.S Foreign Policy in the Middle East." Power and Terror: Conflict,

Hegemony, and the Rule of Terror. Ed. John Junkerman and Takei Masakazu. Pluto.

2011. pp.169 - 196.

Cohen-Mor, Dalya (Editor). "Introduction" Arab Women Writers: An Anthology of Short Stories.

New York State UP. 2005.

Datta, Nonica. Violence, Martyrdom and Partition: A Daughter's Testimony. Oxford India, 2012.

Flip, Sahim and Tahiti Uluc. " Contemporary Turkish

Thought" in The Blackwell Companion to
Contemporary Islamic Thought. Ed. Ibrahim M. Abu-Rabi.
Blackwell. 2006.
Frye, Northrop: "Conclusion to A Literary History of
Canada" The Bush Garden: Essays on
the Canadian Imagination. Anansi. 1971.
Goldie, Terry. Fear and temptation: the image of the
indigene in Canadian, Australian, and New
Zealand literatures. McGill-Queen's Press-MQUP, 1993.
Klooss, Wolfgang. Ed. Across the Lines: Intertextuality and
Transcultural Communication in the
New Literatures in English. Rodopi. 1998.
Laachir, Karima, and Saeed Talajooy, eds. Resistance in
contemporary Middle Eastern cultures:
Literature, cinema and music. Vol. 44. Routledge, 2013.
Luckhurst, Mary, ed. A Companion to Modern British and
Irish Drama 1880-2005. Blackwell.
2006
Mikhail, Mona N. "Middle Eastern Literature and the
Conditions of Modernity: An Introduction."
World Literature Today 60.2 (1986): 197-199.
Parrinder, Patrick. "On Englishness and the Twenty first
Century Novel" The Nation and Novel:
The English Novels from its Origins to the Present Day.
Oxford UP. 2006.
https://in.1947partitionarchive.org/

Acknowledgements

The book is for educational purpose only

Prologue

The idea of this book came from our previous knowledge and inability to get source texts for post graduation studies. We bring forward this text so that students may have this text with them while learning from the new syllabus. This is also to avoid the wastage of printing and xeroxing through which innumerable quantity of papers are wasted into environment. I hope each of you will benefit from this and give us your valuable feedback in amazon and flipkart

Thanking you

Team Papyrus

CHAPTER I

Sleepless I Kept the Night's Vigil Al–Khansaa

Sleepless I Kept the Night's Vigil

- Al-Khansaa
Sleepless I kept the night vigil,
Eyes khol-blackened ruts.
I watched the stars, though no watchman,
Me, wrapped in wragged robes.
For I had heard news- and no news for joy-
Word of you:
'Here is Sakhr,
hurled to the ground, skirted by stones.'
Go then, to God's care,
You whose heart quickened at wrong,
You like the spear-tip
Whose bright shape lit the night,
You, bitterly resolved, free-born,
and the son of the free- Go!
I will weep for you
So long as the ring-dove wails
And stars brighten
The road for the traveller.
And I will not make peace with a people you were at war with,
not till the good host's black pot whitens.
About the Poet

Tumāḍir bint ʿAmr ibn al-Ḥārith ibn al-Sharīd al-Sulamīyah was a 7ᵗʰ-century tribeswoman, living in the Arabian Peninsula. She was one of the most influential poets of the pre-Islamic and early Islamic periods.

In her time, the role of a female poet was to write elegies for the dead and perform them for the tribe in public oral competitions. Al-Khansāʾ won respect and fame in these competitions with her elegies, and is widely considered as the finest author of Arabic elegies and one of the greatest and best known female Arab poets of all time.In 629, she went to Medina with a deputation from her clan and, after meeting the Islamic prophet Muhammad, embraced the new religion. Some say al-Khansāʾ was Muhammad's favorite poet. He wept when he heard her elegies for her two brothers, Ṣakhr and Muʿāwiyah. Her poetry was later recorded by Muslim scholars, who were studying unaltered Arabic of her time in order to explicate the language of early Islamic texts.

The poems of al-Khansāʾ are short and marked by a strong and traditional sense of despair at the irrevocable loss of life. Her style and expression, which assured her a superiority in this genre, became stereotyped in the later rithāʾ poetry. As an outstanding poet and female figure in the history of Arabic literature, the position of al-Khansāʾ is unique. Al-Khansa's elegies were later collected by Ibn al-Sikkit (802–858 CE), a literary scholar of the early Abbasid era. Nearly a thousand lines of her poetry remain.

CHAPTER II

A Woman like Me

A Woman like Me (From A Red Cherry on a White-Tiled Floor)

- Maram Al-Massri
   Women like me
do not know how to speak.
A word remains in their throats
like a thorn
they choose to swallow.
Women like me
know nothing except weeping,
impossible weeping
suddenly
pouring
like a severed artery.
Women like me
receive blows
and do not dare return them.
They shake with anger,
they subdue it.
Like lions in cages,
women like me
dream . . .
of freedom . . .
   About the poet
   Maram al-Massri was born in Lattakia, Syria, to a family
of artists and studied English literature at the University of

Damascus. She worked as an interpreter in Lattakia before moving to Paris, where she has lived since 1982. In 1984 she published her first book of poems, I Threaten You with a White Dove, followed by A Red Cherry on a White-Tiled Floor. Her work has been awarded many prizes and translated into several languages. She has three children.

CHAPTER III

Arab Women Writers: A Brief Sketch

Arab Women Writers: A Brief Sketch

-Dalya Cohen-Mor

Dalya Cohen-Mor (Editor). "Arab women writers: A Brief Sketch".

(Arab Women Writers: An Anthology of Short Stories. New York State UP. 2005. Pp 3-7)

Arab Women Writers: A Brief Sketch

Women in the Arab world have been producing significant fiction for the past half-century. Although the Arabic literary tradition had its narrative types, the short story and the novel were new genres adopted from the West in the late nineteenth and early twentieth centuries. Introduced during the process of cultural revival known in Arabic as al-nahda, the new forms underwent considerable experimentation before gaining acceptance and reaching maturity. The emergence of the short story in particular is closely connected with the development of the Arabic press, which offered authors an avenue of publication and thus a readership. Since the Second World War, when most Arab countries have gained their political independence and their newly formed governments have pursued policies of social and economic reforms, there has been a gradual improvement in the condition of women. The spread of free compulsory public education not only raised the level of literacy among women but also opened the door to new employment opportunities.

Women's participation in public life increased, reaching into all areas of activity. In the domain of literature, women advanced gradually from the margins to the center of literary production and their contribution to modern Arabic literature has been invaluable. Fiction, which possesses the guise of fantasy and therefore entails a lesser degree of exposure and accountability, has become the most popular and powerful vehicle of self-expression and social criticism for women. In the last halfcentury, Arab women writers have brought the art of storytelling to a high level of accomplishment and achieved a remarkable development in theme, form, and technique. Prominent among the pioneer authors are the Palestinian Mayy Ziyada (1886–1941), the Egyptian Suhayr al-Qalamawi (1911–97), and the Syrian Ulfat al-Idilbi (b. 1912).

While the presence of women on the Arabic literary scene has grown in number and influence in recent decades, there are still fewer female than male authors. In addition, they do not represent all segments of Arab society. Most of these women writers come from the middle and upper classes and have had the education and resources needed for intellectual pursuits. In a developing part of the world where illiteracy is still widespread, and where the overwhelming majority of women are preoccupied with the harsh realities of daily life, Virginia Woolf's basic assumption that "a woman must have money and a room of her own if she is to write fiction"2 is of particular relevance. As Woolf elaborates, "Fiction, imaginative work that is, is not dropped like a pebble upon the ground, as science may be; fiction is like a spider's web, attached ever so lightly perhaps, but still attached to life at all four corners.... These webs are not spun in mid-air by incorporeal creatures, but are the work of suffering human beings, and are attached to grossly material things, like health and money and the houses we live in."3 Owing to the privileged social background of most Arab women writers, their fictional works give inadequate attention to, and lack realistic solutions for, the plight of women from the poorer classes of society.4 Despite the increase in the number of women who are creative writers, only very few of them can devote themselves entirely to their writing. Family obligations, full-time jobs, or financial pressures are usually the factors that impede them. It should be noted that the writing of fiction in the Arab world is not a profession by which a person, male or female, can earn a living.

Even the Nobel Prize laureate Naguib Mahfouz worked as a civil servant in Egypt's Ministry of Culture until his retirement. Of the women writers included in this volume, Nawal al-Saadawi, for example, has maintained a dual career as a physician and a writer. Radwa Ashour is a university professor, as were Suhayr al-Qalamawi and Latifa al-Zayyat. Aliya Mamdouh, Fawziya Rashid, Mona Ragab, Fadila al-Faruq, and Hadiya Sa'id are journalists. Ramziya Abbas al-Iryani is a career diplomat. The literary activities of these authors are conducted alongside their duties as wives, mothers, and working women. Economic freedom, however, does not necessarily entail intellectual freedom. Arab women who have had the opportunity to embark on a writing career may still encounter opposition to their work, and may even find it impossible to publish it or acquire a readership. Nawal al-Saadawi published her first work of nonfiction, Women and Sex, in Beirut in 1972. The book deals candidly with taboos surrounding female sexuality, including virginity, circumcision, and crimes of honor. It caused such an uproar that she was dismissed from her post as Egypt's director-general of health education. As with other provocative works that she has penned, the book has been banned in several Arab countries. Layla Ba'labakki of Lebanon published her collection of short stories,

A Spaceship of Tenderness to the Moon, in Beirut in 1963. The book led to her trial on charges of obscenity and endangering public morality.5 The indictment was based on erotic descriptions that appeared in some of her stories. Although she was eventually acquitted, she stopped publishing works of fiction since then. Suhayr al-Tall of Jordan went through a traumatic experience following the publication of her story "The Gallows," included in this anthology, in Amman in 1987. The narrative, a surrealistic depiction of a public execution in which the hangman's noose is portrayed as a huge phallus, landed her in court on a charge of offending public sensibilities. After a long and bitter trial, she was convicted, fined, and sentenced to short imprisonment.6 Zabya Khamis of the United Arab Emirates suffered an even harsher ordeal. In 1987 she was arrested in Abu Dhabi and jailed for five months without trial as punishment for writing allegedly transgressive poetry.7 Besides problems of censorship, Arab women writers may also encounter opposition to their work within their own families. Alifa Rifaat was discouraged from writing first by her father and then by her husband, who threatened her with divorce to enforce his will. Only after his death could she write and publish freely. Nawal al-Saadawi chose to divorce two husbands who were hostile to her literary activities. In most instances, the attitudes of family members— particularly fathers and husbands—whether progressive or conservative, play a critical role in shaping a woman's writing career. The critic and writer Yusuf al-

Sharuni cites the following explanation of this state of affairs in his introduction to The 1002nd Night, the first anthology of short stories by Egyptian women: "Man, especially in our Middle Eastern milieu, does not object to woman's emergence into public life in order to work alongside him, especially if this work relieves him of the burden of bearing the family's living costs by himself. But beyond that he strongly objects to her having an independent social existence, just as he totally rejects the idea of the home becoming a secondary occupation for her, subordinate to her outside, wider world. In other words, man still asserts that the home, not external society, is woman's domain."8 The sociologist Fatima Mernissi has another explanation. In Doing Daily Battle, she writes about her experiences "as a Moroccan woman who uses writing and analysis—two tools which are exclusively male in our culture. And let no one tell me that 'in our heritage there have always been women scholars.' "9 Mernissi states, with an engaging sense of humor, that she has learned to distinguish "the varieties of terrorist tactics that men, who monopolize the symbolic values of our society, use to stop me from expressing myself, or to denigrate what I say—which comes to the same thing." She identifies two main "terrorist tactics": "Firstly, 'What you are talking about is an imported idea' (referring to access to the cultural heritage); and secondly, 'What you are saying is not representative' (referring to access to science)." Debunking these myths, Mernissi comes to the conclusion that "the relations between the sexes are always inextricably and unconditionally linked to class relations."10 From the beginning, then, Arab women writers have had to assert themselves in a male-dominated arena, from audience to publishers to critics to literary tradition.11 The Egyptian author Salwa Bakr acknowledges the formidable task facing an Arab woman writer: "It is a heavy tax on many levels, especially in a society in which most individuals are illiterate, a society which is conservative by nature, whose values are static and which does not respect women in the first place.

All this makes writing seem like the task of Sisyphus, particularly if the writer stops to think for whom she is writing."12 Yet despite the various obstacles that they encounter in the path of their careers, Arab women writers continue to give literary expression to their feelings and thoughts. Many of the authors presented in this anthology have produced a large volume of work and achieved eminence, among them Ulfat al-Idilbi (Syria), Hanan alShaykh (Lebanon), Layla al-Uthman (Kuwait), Nawal al-Saadawi (Egypt), and Daisy al-Amir (Iraq). Others, such as Samiya At'ut (Palestine), Nuzha Bin Sulayman (Morocco), Umayma al-Khamis (Saudi Arabia), and Sahar al-Muji (Egypt) are rising young writers. While most of the established authors have also received international recognition by being translated into European languages, for several of the new authors, this volume marks their first appearance in English. Two groups of women writers can be distinguished in this anthology: those from the Arab East (Mashriq), and those from the Arab West (Maghrib). Historically and culturally, these parts of the Arab world have developed differently. Domination by European colonial powers in the nineteenth and twentieth centuries contributed to this division. The countries of the Arab East were mostly under British colonial rule (e.g., Egypt, Palestine, Iraq), while those of the Arab West (e.g., Algeria, Tunisia, Morocco) were largely occupied by the French.

French colonial rule explains the problem of biculturalism facing North African writers.13 Whereas British colonial policy did not impose the English language and culture on the colonized, the French embarked on an aggressive linguistic and cultural campaign that sought to replace the indigenous languages and cultures. The result has been the emergence of whole generations of intellectuals who are francophones and prefer to express themselves in French. The Algerian women writers Jamila Debeche and Assia Djebar, their male counterparts Muhammed Dib and Kateb Yacine, as well as the Moroccan novelist Driss Chraibi and the Tunisian Albert Memmi, all illustrate this phenomenon. It is interesting to note that North African authors who choose to write in Arabic occasionally show traces of French influence in their diction. For example, the Moroccan writer Khannatha Bannuna in her story "Suqut al-intizar" (Shattered Expectations) uses the phrase 'ilab allayl to mean "night clubs," which is a word-for-word translation from the French boîtes de nuit. 14 Similarly, the Algerian Fadila al-Faruq, in the story "Homecoming," uses the word miziriyya (French: misère) for "misery." On the whole, while the majority of literary works coming from the Arab East are in Arabic, those coming from North Africa are in French. In this volume, only women writers of Arabic have been included.

Scribbling Notes

CHAPTER IV

The Sultan's Dilemma

The Sultan's Dilemma

-Tawfik Al-Hakim

Tawfik Al-Hakim (1899 – 1987)•He marks the real beginnings & development of modern Arabic drama•He is the founder of Arabic drama•He adapted European plays•Introduced social & political issues of the time:the nationalist struggle & theemancipation of women which he ridiculed.•His legal service in different parts of the country provided him withinteresting experience & hence valuable material for his creative writing•The Sleepers in the Cave (1933)•The Sultan's Dilemma (1960)•The founder of drama in Arabic.•Studied stage in France.•Adapted European plays.•His plays are divided into:•Comedy of Manners & Themes from Society•Drama of Ideas: Ahl al-Kahf•Criticism of Society•Post-1952 Revolution: The Sultan's Dilemma•The Absurd & Disillusion•Drama of IdeasSleepers in the Cave (1933)T. Husayn commented on Al-Hakim: 'the first work in Arabic literature whichmay be properly called drama'.•When first performed in 1935 failed.•Theater of the mind/ideas did not appeal to people.•It is a full-length, four-act play.

At the time of Tawfiq al-Hakim's birth, Egypt was under Ottoman rule. In 1881 a military mutiny, led by Colonel Ahmed Arabi, took place against the Khedive (a title given to the Turkish viceroys ruling Egypt from 1867 to 1914). Arabi demanded a popularly-elected legislature and an increased budget for the army. The movement began among the Egyptian officers, who complained of the preference shown to officers of Turkish origin.

The mutiny then expanded into an attack on the privileged position and predominant influence of foreigners and the European interference in Egyptian affairs. A British expeditionary force landed at both ends of the Suez Canal in August 1882. The Egyptian army was defeated and the Ottoman Khedive Tawfiq was restored to power. This marked the beginning of British military occupation of Egypt that lasted until 1936. Between 1892 and 1914, however, Turkey still held power. Following Khedive Tawfiq's death in 1892 his son Abbas Helmy II assumed the title of Khedive. Abbas Helmy ruled until his dethronement in 1914 when Egypt was proclaimed a British protectorate. Tawfiq al-Hakim was born at his aunt's house in his mother's home town of Alexandria. His father was away from home on a legal assignment at the time of the birth. Al-Hakim's uncle wrote, "I saw him this morning, and found him to be like his father - except that he had no mustache!" (al-Hakim, Prison 4).

As al-Hakim's father was not present at the birth, his mother chose his name, Husayn Tawfiq al-Hakim. Tawfiq al-Hakim's father, Isma'il al-Hakim, was not from a wealthy family and lived solely on his earnings as a prosecutor. Isma'il had been one of the best students in his class at Law School and, with some fellow students, had founded the school Law Journal. He was widely-read not only in his legal texts and the Qu'ran but also literature, particularly classical poetry and narrative prose. However, following his marriage to a haughty and strong-willed woman, Isma'il apparently abandoned his literary pursuits (Starkey, 16, 17). Isma'il's marriage to al-Hakim's mother had been arranged by his step-mother who sent his aunt and sister to her home town of Alexandria to look for a wife. Despite the small dowry being offered, and, against the objections of her mother, the prospective bride was impressed with Isma'il's photograph and legal position and the match was struck. Isma'il earned various promotions in his legal position with the government, from Associate Prosecutor to Prosecutor. The resulting assignments around the countryside, however, meant that the family was constantly on the move. Al-Hakim never named his mother in his autobiography, though Richard Long has identified her as Asma al-Bustami (Long 1). Her family descended from Turkish, Persian or Albanian seafarers. She had a strong personality and spent much of her childhood quarrelling with her only sibling, a sister. Their mother was a widow, who married her widowed brother-in-law and united the two families. Al-Hakim's mother learned to read and write due, in part, to one of her step-brothers who would tell her tales from a/f /ai/a wa/ai/a (Arabian Nights). This step-brother also persuaded his father to hire a Qu'ranic tutor for her. Once she learned the alphabet she was able to read the tales for herself. This set her apart from most other women of this era, as it was not the norm for women to be able to read and write.

After her marriage to Isma'il al-Hakim in the 1890s she joined her new husband in al-Mahalia al-Kubra. It was only when she saw her bare home that she found out about his meager salary. However, Isma'il was soon promoted to Prosecuting Agent, 4th Level at a higher salary. Despite their improved financial situation, al-Hakim's mother wanted her own financial independence. She had a small private income from her own side of the family which she used to invest in some land. She was furious, however, to discover that Isma'il had registered only part of the land in her name, placing the remainder in his own name. Conditions in the household were difficult until Isma'il relented and reregistered the entire property in her name. A few months after Tawfiq al-Hakim was born, the family went to visit Isma'il's father hoping he might offer some financial help. An argument ensued between Isma'il's wife and his step-mother. Isma'il's wife refused to apologize, so Ismail "pulled her away by the hand, either muttering the formula of repudiation or threatening her with it" (al-Hakim, Prison 35). Under some schools of Islamic law, a husband has only to utter his intention to repudiate his wife three times for a divorce to become legally binding. The situation was finally resolved by Isma'il's father, who was secretly impressed with her courage in going up against the lady of the house.

As a young adult, al-Hakim was skeptical about marriage, probably because of the state of his parents' marriage and the dominant role which his mother played in the marriage. Al-Hakim considered his father dull, with no trace of his youthful exuberance. Al-Hakim believed his father's subservient behaviour was due to his mother's rebellious, aggressive, personality "that directed her husband's development the way she wanted it, that confined his energy within the material family frame-work" (al-Hakim, Prison 26, 27.) His mother tried to persuade al-Hakim otherwise, but he persisted in his belief. Apparently this experience with his mother kept him from marrying until later in life. It is probable that the state of his parents' marriage would affect his writing in later life and would add misogyny as one of the recurring themes in his plays. Richard Long agrees that at "an early age the seeds of misogyny were sewn" (Long 3), seeds that would show up in later in his works. Isma'il and his wife had a second son. This time Isma'il was present for the birth and chose his son's name, Zuhayr in honour of the pre-islamic poet Zuhayr ibn Abi Sulma. His wife was ill after giving birth but soon improved. When the boys grew older they shared a bed. The two boys were as different in their personalities as were their parents. While Zuhayr's personality was like his mother's, al-Hakim's was more like that of his father. Ismail had an extremely careful and precise personality. He kept a notebook in which he wrote important facts, diary entries and items of concern; he carried a pocket watch which he set back ten minutes so that "he would always have ten minutes to spare for emergencies"

BACKGROUND OF THE PLAY

The period spanning from High Medieval period to Late Medieval period witnessed many changes in the interaction between religion and politics both in Europe, Asia and in the Middle East. In Africa, the rise of alien belief-systems on the pretext of civilization affected the prevailing conditions of politics. These manifested in the thematic occupations of the dramas of this era. Among the many works that evolve during the modern Arabic era, the dramas of Tewfiq al-Hakim is noted for its revolutionary impulse to shake up the status quo by exposing the gaps that exist in the social and religious order. These impulses are evoked by deep philosophical thoughts arising from the point of consciousness and are used to resolve dramatic conflicts. The Sultan's Dilemma is an archetype of the mindfulness of the collusion between belief-system and politics. Tawfiq Al- Hakim's The Sultan's Dilemma (TSD) is a comedy written in 1960. It revolves around a Sultan from the Mamluk system who knew that the people in his city say that he is still a slave and that his previous master did not properly manumit him. According to them, The

Sultan has no right to rule or be the ruler before becoming free. The Sultan vacillates between using forces to silence people (the minister's opinion) and following the law (and this is the judge's opinion). He, therefore, decided to follow the law and has himself sold by auction with the condition that his new owner will then set him free. However, the play is not a historical play, for it deals with timeless problems. The Mameluk era was known for its spread of violence, bribery, conspiracy, and deception and injustice in Egypt. The critic Fatima Yusuf Muhammad (as cited in Saqer, 2011) believes that Al-Hakim has chosen to return to that history to escape authority censorship at his time.

Nevertheless, he symbolically carried on the intellectual connotations and political projections. He expressed his opinion on the spoiled democracy aftermath of the Revolution of 1952, where its atmosphere was closer to the Mameluk. Moreover, the play sheds light not only on the conflict between the power of law and force. It examines how men of strength twist the law as a means of justice to agree with our daily practices. In this play, Al-Hakim got inspiration from his work as a judge and his awareness of the judicial system's varied practices.

In his introduction to the play, Al-Hakim claims a correlation between the play's events and Egypt's political scenes after the revolution in1952. Then, the country was under totalitarian emergency power and the military Junta. In a book entitled Tawfiq Al-Hakim: A Reader's Guide, Hutchins (2003) argues that this play is Al-Hakim's message to Abdel Nasser not to behave as he desired and that he had to submit to the law. The play's opening scene is met with a comic treatment of the idea of human rights and freedom of expression in a society ruled by a totalitarian system. Just like the graveyard scene in Hamlet, an

Executioner and a Condemned Man, who is an "old slave-trader", banter about the impending death sentence, toasting the Condemned Man's health and Executioner's masterful work of beheading

Scribbling Notes

CHAPTER V

Purdah I

Purdah I

-Imtiaz Dharker

One day they said
she was old enough to learn some shame.
She found it came quite naturally.

Purdah is a kind of safety.
The body finds a place to hide.
The cloth fans out against the skin
much like the earth that falls
on coffins after they put dead men in.

People she has known
stand up, sit down as they have always done.
But they make different angles
in the light, their eyes aslant,
a little sly.

She half-remembers things
from someone else's life,
perhaps from yours, or mine –
carefully carrying what we do not own:
between the thighs a sense of sin.

We sit still, letting the cloth grow
a little closer to our skin.

A light filters inward
through our bodies' walls.
Voices speak inside us,
echoing in the places we have just left.

She stands outside herself,
sometimes in all four corners of a room.
Wherever she goes, she is always
inching past herself,
as if she were a clod of earth
and the roots as well,
scratching for a hold
between the first and second rib.

Passing constantly out of her own hands,
into the corner of someone else's eyes . . .
while the doors keep opening
inward and again
inward.

From: Purdah

Publisher: Oxford University Press, Delhi

About the Poet

Dharker is a poet, artist and video film-maker. She was awarded the Queen's Gold Medal for Poetry in 2014.She received the Cholmondeley Award and an Honorary Doctorate from SOAS, and is a Fellow of the Royal Society of Literature. In 2020 she became the Chancellor of Newcastle University. Her collections include Purdah (Oxford University Press), Postcards from god, I speak for the devil and The terrorist at my table (all published by Penguin India and Bloodaxe Books UK), Leaving Fingerprints, Over the Moon and the latest, Luck is the Hook (Bloodaxe Books UK). Her poems are on the British

GCSE and A Level English syllabus, and she reads with other poets at Poetry Live! events all over the country to more than 25,000 students a year. She has been Poet in Residence at Cambridge University Library, worked on a series of poems based on the Archives of St Paul's Cathedral as well as projects across art forms in Leeds, Newcastle and Hull. The inaugural Poet of the Fair at London Book Fair, her poems have been broadcast widely on BBC Radio 3 and 4 as well as the BBC World Service. She has had eleven solo exhibitions of drawings in India, London, New York and Hong Kong. She scripts and directs films, many of them for non-government organisations in India, working in the area of shelter, education and health for women and children.

CHAPTER VI

She Is

She Is

-Tsering Wangmo Dhompa

Her voice is a roundness. On full moon days, she talks about

renouncing meat but the butcher has his routine. And blood.

M's wisdom. Still reliable.

There are sounds we cannot hear but understand in motion.

Slicing of air with hips. Crushing grass, saying these are my feet.

I want my feet in my shadow. Suffice to meet desires halfway.

Quiet. We say her chakras are in place.

When the thermos shatters, she knows the direction of its spill.

She knows how to lead and follow. Know her from this.

Sounds we cannot hear. The wind blows and we say it is cool.

Night slips under the door. We are tucked into bed and

kissed

a fleeting one. Through the curtains, her voice loosens like thread

from an old blanket, row upon row. We watch her teeth in the

dark and read her words. She speaks in perfect order, facing where

the breeze can tug it towards canals stretching for sound.

Her faith abides by the cycle of the moon. See how perfect she is.

Tsering Wangmo Dhompa, "She is" from Rules of the House. Copyright © 2003 by Tsering Wangmo Dhompa. Reprinted by permission of Apogee Press.

Source: Rules of the House (Apogee Press, 2003)

About the poet

Tsering Wangmo Dhompa is the first Tibetan female poet to be published in English. She was raised in India and Nepal. Tsering received her BA from Lady Shri Ram College, University of Delhi. She pursued her MA from University of Massachusetts and her MFA in creative writing from San Francisco State University. She has a Ph.D. in literature from the University of California, Santa Cruz and is currently an assistant professor in the English Department at Villanova University. Her first book of poems, Rules of the House, published by Apogee Press in 2002, was a finalist for the Asian American Literary Awards in 2003. Other publications include, most recently a chapbook Revolute (Albion Books, 2021),My Rice Tastes Like the Lake (Apogee Press 2011), In the Absent Everyday (also from Apogee Press), and two chapbooks: In Writing the Names (A.bacus, Poets & Poets Press) and Recurring Gestures (Tangram Press). In Letter For Love she delivered her first short story. In 2013, Penguin India published Tsering's first full-length book, A Home in Tibet, in which she chronicles her successive journeys to Tibet and provides ethnographic details of ordinary Tibetans inside Tibet.

CHAPTER VII

Political Science

Political Science

(Ko Ko Thett)

A tongue that demands 'Water! Water! Water!' is chapped

from tonguing the thick lips of a totalitarian ashtray.

You may find life in a bombshell. There is no water in ash.

They redress their national internal bleeding with quacky tincture. There's no cure for national internal bleeding.

To tame the tsunami they whip the ocean with a knout. The ocean doesn't bother.

"On this land ...", Their slogan goes, "... there's no corpse who died from starvation!" . Infants who were force-fed that shrunk into skin-on bones carcasses.

Drought makes you think, thieve, and thrive.

"Moderation is medicine, excess—poison." lectures a baton

blow on a citizen.

Some of us love flexural history. Others make do with bitter rainwater.

.

.

Ko Ko Thett's commentary on "Political Science": Drought makes you think, thieve and thrive. It is a hike in petrol prices or the removal of certain privileges that drives people to the streets. Then again, there's only so much people can do in their struggle against tyranny. Compare an army with a mob. The former is a solid institution and the latter, a transient community. The only language a gun will understand may be bang-bang. They say mass protests should emulate water in undermining rock-solid oppressive institutions. The question is how long does it take? How much human sacrifice? Human sacrifice has its limits. Human life is fragile and short. Look at the UK, the country that boasts the oldest democratic foundations, that same country is also partly run by a racist monarchy. Even with guns, to paraphrase Ursula Le Guin, we may have won the war, but have we really defeated Hitlerism anywhere?

About the Poet

Ko Ko Thett is a Burma-born poet, poetry editor, translator, and anthologist of contemporary Burmese poetry. His poems have appeared in journals worldwide (from Griffith Review to Granta), and translated into several languages. After a whirlwind tour of Asia, Europe and North America for two decades, Ko Ko happily resettled in Sagaing in his native Burma-Myanmar in 2017. As of 2021 he is most likely to be spotted in the Golden Triangle area of Norwich, UK. He writes in both Burmese and English.

CHAPTER VIII

Bullocky

Bullocky

Judith Wright

    Beside his heavy-shouldered team
thirsty with drought and chilled with rain,
he weathered all the striding years
till they ran widdershins in his brain:

Till the long solitary tracks
etched deeper with each lurching load
were populous before his eyes,
and fiends and angels used his road.

All the long straining journey grew
a mad apocalyptic dream,
and he old Moses, and the slaves
his suffering and stubborn team.

Then in his evening camp beneath
the half-light pillars of the trees
he filled the steepled cone of night
with shouted prayers and prophecies.

While past the campfire's crimson ring
the star struck darkness cupped him round.
and centuries of cattle-bells
rang with their sweet uneasy sound.

Grass is across the wagon-tracks,
and plough strikes bone beneath the grass,
and vineyards cover all the slopes
where the dead teams were used to pass.

O vine, grow close upon that bone
and hold it with your rooted hand.
The prophet Moses feeds the grape,
and fruitful is the Promised Land.

Judith Wright was a prolific Australian poet, critic, and short-story writer, who published more than 50 books. Wright was also an uncompromising environmentalist and social activist campaigning for Aboriginal land rights. She believed that the poet should be concerned with national and social problems. At the age of 85, just before her death, she attended in Canberra at a march for reconciliation with Aboriginal people.

About the poet

Judith Wright was born in Armidale, New South Wales. The eldest child of Phillip Wright and his first wife, Ethel, she spent most of her formative years in Brisbane and Sydney.Wright was of Cornish ancestry. After the early death of her mother, she lived with her aunt and then boarded at New England Girls' School after her father's remarriage in 1929. After graduating, Wright studied Philosophy, English, Psychology and History at the University of Sydney. At the beginning of World War II, she returned to her father's station (ranch) to help during the shortage of labour caused by the war.

CHAPTER IX

Waltzing Matilda

Waltzing Matilda

-Andrew Barton Paterson

Oh there once was a swagman camped in the billabong,
Under the shade of a Coolabah tree;
And he sang as he looked at his old billy boiling
"Who'll come a-waltzing Matilda with me."

Who'll come a-waltzing Matilda, my darling.
Who'll come a-waltzing Matilda with me.
Waltzing Matilda and leading a water-bag —
Who'll come a-waltzing Matilda with me.

Down came a jumbuck to drink at the waterhole,
Up jumped the swagman and grabbed him in glee;
And he sang as he stowed him away in his tucker-bag,
"You'll come a-waltzing Matilda with me."

Who'll come a-waltzing Matilda, my darling.
Who'll come a-waltzing Matilda with me.
Waltzing Matilda and leading a water-bag —
Who'll come a-waltzing Matilda with me.

Down came the squatter a-riding his thoroughbred;
Down came policemen — one, two, and three.
"Whose is the jumbuck you've got in the tucker-bag?
You'll come a-waltzing Matilda with we."

Who'll come a-waltzing Matilda, my darling.
Who'll come a-waltzing Matilda with me.
Waltzing Matilda and leading a water-bag —
Who'll come a-waltzing Matilda with me.

But the swagman, he up and he jumped in the waterhole,
Drowning himself by the Coolabah tree;
And his ghost may be heard as it sings in the billabong
"Who'll come a-waltzing Matilda with me?"

Who'll come a-waltzing Matilda, my darling.
Who'll come a-waltzing Matilda with me.
Waltzing Matilda and leading a water-bag.
Who'll come a-waltzing Matilda with me.

About the poet

Andrew Barton "Banjo" Paterson, CBE[1] (17 February 1864 – 5 February 1941)[2] was an Australian bush poet, journalist and author. He wrote many ballads and poems about Australian life, focusing particularly on the rural and outback areas, including the district around Binalong, New South Wales, where he spent much of his childhood. Paterson's more notable poems include "Clancy of the Overflow" (1889), "The Man from Snowy River" (1890) and "Waltzing Matilda" (1895), regarded widely as Australia's unofficial national anthem

CHAPTER X

Jews in the Land of Israel

Jews in the Land of Israel

- Yehuda Amichai
TRANSLATED BY CHANA BLOCH
We forget where we came from. Our Jewish
names from the Exile give us away,
bring back the memory of flower and fruit, medieval
cities,
metals, knights who turned to stone, roses,
spices whose scent drifted away, precious stones, lots of
red,
handicrafts long gone from the world
(the hands are gone too).
Circumcision does it to us,
as in the Bible story of Shechem and the sons of Jacob,
so that we go on hurting all our lives.
What are we doing, coming back here with this pain?
Our longings were drained together with the swamps,
the desert blooms for us, and our children are beautiful.
Even the wrecks of ships that sank on the way
reached this shore,
even winds did. Not all the sails.
What are we doing
in this dark land with its
yellow shadows that pierce the eyes?
(Every now and then someone says, even after forty
or fifty years: "The sun is killing me.")

What are we doing with these souls of mist, with these names,
with our eyes of forests, with our beautiful children,
with our quick blood?
Spilled blood is not the roots of trees
but it's the closest thing to roots
we have.
Yehuda Amichai, "Jews in the Land of Israel" from The Poetry of Yehuda Amichai. Copyright © 2015 by Yehuda Amichai. Reprinted by permission of Hana Amichai.
Source: The Poetry of Yehuda Amichai (Farrar Straus and Giroux, 2015)
About the poet
Yehuda Amichai was an Israeli poet and author, one of the first to write in colloquial Hebrew in modern times. Amichai was awarded the 1957 Shlonsky Prize, the 1969 Brenner Prize, 1976 Bialik Prize, and 1982 Israel Prize. He also won international poetry prizes, and was nominated several times for the Nobel Prize in Literature.

CHAPTER XI

Of Course, It Hurts

Of Course, It Hurts

Karin Boyes

Of course it hurts when buds burst.

Otherwise why would spring hesitate?

Why would all our fervent longing be bound in the frozen bitter haze?

The bud was the casing all winter.

What is this new thing, which consumes and bursts?

Of course it hurts when buds burst,

pain for that which grows and for that which envelops.

Of course it is hard when drops fall.

Trembling with fear they hang heavy,

clammer on the branch,

swell and slide - the weight pulls them down,

how they cling.

Hard to be uncertain, afraid and divided,

hard to feel the deep pulling and calling,

yet sit there and just quiver

- hard to want to stay and to want to fall.

Then, at the point of agony and when all is beyond help,

the tree's buds burst as if in jubilation,

then, when fear no longer exists,

the branch's drops tumble in a shimmer,

forgetting that they were afraid of the new,

forgetting that they were fearful of the journey

- feeling for a second their greatest security,

resting in the trust that creates the world.
Translated into English by Jenny Nunn in "To a friend".

Swedish original

About the poet

Karin Maria Boye was a Swedish poet and novelist. In Sweden she is acclaimed as a poet, but internationally she is best known for the dystopian science fiction novel Kallocain (1940).

CHAPTER XII

At the city pound

At the city pound

Vincent O'Sullivan

I'm in charge of a cage. I know those that won't.
I don't mean can't. Just won't. There's a roster
for Tuesdays, Fridays. Dogs to die.
The disconsolate, the abandoned, those with recurrent
symptoms, the incorrigible mutt — oh, a dozen
choices by way of reasons. Even so,
some won't. Won't play along once their number's
up. The "rainbow bridge" in the offing
as the posher clinics put it, a pig's ear
as a final treat, a venison chew, the profession
behaving beautifully at a time like this.
Still, those that won't. Won't go nicely, I mean,
with a gaze to melt, a last slobbed lick.
Those with a soul's defiance, though embarrassment
in the lunchroom should you come at that one!
Even after the bag is zipped, you feel it:
We're real at the end as you are, buster. We sniff
the wind. What say if we say it together? Won't.

About the Poet

Sir Vincent Gerard O'Sullivan KNZM (born 28 September 1937) is one of New Zealand's best-known writers. He is a poet, short story writer, novelist, playwright, critic, editor, biographer, and librettist.O'Sullivan lectured at Victoria University of

Wellington (VUW) from 1963 to 1966, and the University of Waikato between 1968 and 1978).[3] He served as literary editor of the NZ Listener from 1979 to 1980, and then between 1981 and 1987 won a series of writer's residencies and research fellowships in universities in Australia and New Zealand: VUW, University of Tasmania, Deakin University (Geelong), Flinders University in Adelaide, University of Western Australia, and University of Queensland.These were interrupted in 1983 by a year as resident playwright at Downstage Theatre, Wellington. In 1988 he returned to VUW, where he was professor of English literature until his retirement in 2004.The Dark is Light Enough: Ralph Hotere a Biographical Portrait won for him the 2021 General non-fiction award at the Ockham New Zealand Book Awards

CHAPTER XIII

Attitudes for a New Zealand Poet

Attitudes for a New Zealand Poet

Allen Curnow

That part of you the world offended so
Has strophied, or else your strategy
has changed, or else you have so much to do
The simplest way is seeming to agree
The falling cities, bones and brutal sky,
And Eliot cactuses, do not recur
Now, it is not an easy quaestion why
Yopu were ashamed that things were as they were
Come world, poor Jack-wold, and let us reason
Together, settle down and take our time.
We shall have bomber and bud in the same season,
Music, and malice both in the same rhyme,
Thunder and tears: committed at this stage
Neither to horror nor a horrible age
World, up to now we've heard your hungers wail
No more than mock alerts. An island moon
Unspeckled with our deaths can safely sail,
Escorted by our Never past our Soon
The great sad duchess by a trick saw pass
Shapes of her husband and her children dead:
But further off, darker than in a glass,
The natural body of our grief is read.
About the Poet

Thomas Allen Monro Curnow ONZ CBE (17 June 1911 – 23 September 2001) was a New Zealand poet and journalist.Curnow was born in Timaru, New Zealand, the son of a fourth generation New Zealander, an Anglican clergyman, and he grew up in a religious family. The family was of Cornish origin. Curnow wrote a long-running weekly satirical poetry column under the pen-name of Whim Wham for The Press from 1937, and then The New Zealand Herald from 1951, finishing in 1988 – a far-reaching period in which he turned his keen wit to many world issues, from Franco, Hitler, Vietnam, Apartheid, and the White Australia policy, to the internal politics of Walter Nash and the eras of Robert Muldoon and David Lange, all interspersed with humorous commentary on New Zealand's obsession with rugby and other light-hearted subjects.

CHAPTER XIV

Utopia Poem

Utopia Poem

Wislawa Szymborska
	sland where all becomes clear.
Solid ground beneath your feet.

The only roads are those that offer access.

Bushes bend beneath the weight of proofs.

The Tree of Valid Supposition grows here
with branches disentangled since time immermorial.

The Tree of Understanding, dazzling straight and simple.
sprouts by the spring called Now I Get It.

The thicker the woods, the vaster the vista:
the Valley of Obviously.

If any doubts arise, the wind dispels them instantly.

Echoes stir unsummoned
and eagerly explain all the secrets of the worlds.

On the right a cave where Meaning lies.

On the left the Lake of Deep Conviction.

Truth breaks from the bottom and bobs to the surface.

Unshakable Confidence towers over the valley.
Its peak offers an excellent view of the Essence of Things.

For all its charms, the island is uninhabited,
and the faint footprints scattered on its beaches
turn without exception to the sea.

As if all you can do here is leave
and plunge, never to return, into the depths.

Into unfathomable life.

About the Poet

Maria Wisława Anna Szymborska was a Polish poet, essayist, translator, and recipient of the 1996 Nobel Prize in Literature. Born in Prowent (now part of Kórnik), she resided in Kraków until the end of her life. In Poland, Szymborska's books have reached sales rivaling prominent prose authors', though she wrote in a poem, "Some Like Poetry" ("Niektórzy lubią poezję"), that "perhaps" two in a thousand people like poetry.

Szymborska was awarded the 1996 Nobel Prize in Literature "for poetry that with ironic precision allows the historical and biological context to come to light in fragments of human reality". She became better known internationally as a result. Her work has been translated into English and many European languages, as well as into Arabic, Hebrew, Japanese, Persian and Chinese.

CHAPTER XV

To My Little Girl

To My Little Girl

Zofia Romanowicz

I'll make a set of dishes for my little girl,
I think it will be lovely;
I'll mold goblets,
I'll turn plates,
I'll paint it with wonders,
Suns, stars, birds –
How my little girl will clap her hands!
But if her little hand thoughtlessly
Bumps something and the set shatters,
Don't cry, my little one.
Our life too is fragile!
More fragile than these goblets
With their painted stars –
Do you know – my heart is full of bloody shards . . .

Zofia Romanowicz was arrested by the Nazis in January 1941 and imprisoned for resistance activities. In April 1942 she was deported to Ravensbrück, and in September 1943 she was transferred to Neu-Rohlau. There, while working in a china factory, she wrote the premonitory poem "For My Little Girl . . ." She escaped in the spring of 1945 during an evacuation march and was taken to Rome. In 1946 she settled in Paris. Together with her husband, Kazimierz Romanowicz, they managed the bookstore and publishing house Libella and the Galerie Lambert for nearly fifty years. She wrote eleven novels and numerous short stories and poems. She was awarded the Kościelski Award in 1964 and the Prize of the Polish Ministry of Culture & National Heritage in 2001 for the totality of her work.

Alice-Catherine Carls is Tom Elam Distinguished Professor of History at the University of Tennessee at Martin. An internationally published diplomatic and cultural historian of twentieth-century Europe, she is also a translator and literary critic. She serves on several editorial boards and commissions in the United States and abroad.

Daniel Simon is a poet, essayist, translator, and WLT's assistant director and editor in chief. His most recent edited collection, Dispatches from the Republic of Letters: 50 Years of the Neustadt International Prize for Literature (2020), was nominated for a 2020 Foreword INDIES Award.

Scribbling Notes

CHAPTER XVI

THE HEAVENLY CHRISTMAS TREE

THE HEAVENLY CHRISTMAS TREE

by Fyodor Michailovitch Dostoevsky

I am a novelist, and I suppose I have made up this story. I write "I suppose," though I know for a fact that I have made it up, but yet I keep fancying that it must have happened somewhere at some time, that it must have happened on Christmas Eve in some great town in a time of terrible frost.

I have a vision of a boy, a little boy, six years old or even younger. This boy woke up that morning in a cold damp cellar. He was dressed in a sort of little dressing-gown and was shivering with cold. There was a cloud of white steam from his breath, and sitting on a box in the corner, he blew the steam out of his mouth and amused himself in his dullness watching it float away. But he was terribly hungry. Several times that morning he went up to the plank bed where his sick mother was lying on a mattress as thin as a pancake, with some sort of bundle under her head for a pillow. How had she come here? She must have come with her boy from some other town and suddenly fallen ill. The landlady who let the "corners" had been taken two days before to the police station, the lodgers were out and about as the holiday was so near, and the only one left had been lying for the last twenty-four hours dead drunk, not having waited for Christmas. In another corner of the room a wretched old woman of eighty, who had once been a children's nurse but was now left to die friendless, was moaning and groaning with rheumatism, scolding and grumbling at the boy so that he was afraid to go near her corner. He had got a drink of water in the outer room, but could not find a crust anywhere, and had been on the point of waking his mother a dozen times. He felt frightened at last in the darkness: it had long been dusk, but no light was kindled. Touching his mother's face, he was surprised that she did not move at all and that she was as cold as the wall. "It is very cold here," he thought. He stood a little, unconsciously letting his hands rest on the dead woman's shoulders, then he breathed on his fingers to warm them, and then quietly fumbling for his cap on the bed, he went out of the cellar. He would have gone earlier, but was afraid of the big dog which had been howling all day at the neighbor's door at the top of the stairs. But the dog was not there now, and he went out into the street.

Mercy on us, what a town! He had never seen anything like it before. In the town from which he had come, it was always such black darkness at night. There was one lamp for the whole street, the little, low-pitched, wooden houses were closed up with shutters, there was no one to be seen in the street after dusk, all the people shut themselves up in their houses, and there was nothing but the howling of packs of dogs, hundreds and thousands of them barking and howling all night. But there it was so warm and he was given food, while here—oh dear if he only had something to eat! And what a noise and rattle here, what light and what people, horses and carriages, and what a frost! The frozen steam hung in clouds over the horses, over their warmly breathing mouths; their hoofs clanged against the stones through the powdery snow, and everyone pushed so, and—oh, dear, how he longed for some morsel to eat, and how wretched he suddenly felt. A policeman walked by and turned away to avoid seeing the boy.

Here was another street—oh, what a wide one, here he would be run over for certain; how everyone was shouting, racing and driving along, and the light, the light! And what was this? A huge glass window, and through the window a tree reaching up to the ceiling; it was a fir tree, and on it were ever so many lights, gold papers and apples and little dolls and horses; and there were children clean and dressed in their best running about the room, laughing and playing and eating and drinking something. And then a little girl began dancing with one of the boys, what a pretty little girl! And he could hear the music through the window. The boy looked and wondered and laughed although his toes were aching with the cold and his fingers were red and stiff so that it hurt him to move them. And all at once the boy remembered how his toes and fingers hurt him, and began crying, and ran on, and again through another window-pane he saw another Christmas tree, and on a table cakes of all sorts—almond cakes, red cakes and yellow cakes, and three grand young ladies were sitting there, and they gave the cakes to anyone who went up to them, and the door kept opening, lots of gentlemen and ladies went in from the street. The boy crept up, suddenly opened the door and went in. Oh, how they shouted at him and waved him back! One lady went up to him hurriedly and slipped a kopeck into his hand, and with her own hands opened the door into the street for him! How frightened he was. And the kopeck rolled away and clinked upon the steps; he could not bend his red fingers to hold it tight. The boy ran away and went on, where he did not know. He was ready to cry again, but he was afraid, and ran on and on and blew his fingers. And he was miserable because he felt suddenly so lonely and terrified, and all at once, mercy on us! What was this again? People were standing in a crowd admiring. Behind a glass window there were three little dolls, dressed in red and green dresses, and exactly, exactly as though they were alive. One was a little old man sitting and playing a big violin, the two others were standing close by and playing little violins and nodding in time, and looking at one another, and their lips moved, they were speaking, actually speaking, only one couldn't hear through the glass. And at first, the boy thought they were alive, and when he grasped that they were dolls he laughed. He had never seen such dolls before, and had no idea there were such dolls! And he wanted to cry, but he felt amused, amused by the dolls. All at once he fancied that some one caught at his smock behind: a wicked big boy was standing beside him and suddenly hit him on the head, snatched off his cap and tripped him up. The boy fell down on the ground, at once there was a shout, he was numb with fright, he jumped up and ran away. He ran, and not knowing where he was going, ran in at the gate of some one's courtyard, and sat down behind a stack of wood: "They won't find me here, besides it's dark!"

He sat huddled up and was breathless from fright, and all at once, quite suddenly, he felt so happy: his hands and feet suddenly left off aching and grew so warm, as warm as though he were on a stove; then he shivered all over, then he gave a start, why, he must have been asleep. How nice to have a sleep here! "I'll sit here a little and go and look at the dolls again," said the boy, and smiled thinking of them. "Just as though they were alive!..." And suddenly he heard his mother singing over him. "Mammy, I am asleep; how nice it is to sleep here!"

"Come to my Christmas tree, little one," a soft voice suddenly whispered over his head.

He thought that this was still his mother, but no, it was not she. Who it was calling him, he could not see, but someone bent over and embraced him in the darkness; and he stretched out his hands to him, and ... and all at once—oh, what a bright light! Oh, what a Christmas tree! And yet it was not a fir tree, he had never seen a tree like that! Where was he now? Everything was bright and shining, and all around him were dolls; but no, they were not dolls, they were little boys and girls, only so bright and shining. They all came flying around him, they all kissed him, took him and carried him along with them, and he was flying himself, and he saw that his mother was looking at him and laughing joyfully. "Mammy, Mammy; oh, how nice it is here, Mammy!" And again he kissed the children and wanted to tell them at once of those dolls in the shop window. "Who are you, boys? Who are you, girls?" he asked, laughing and admiring them.

"This is Christ's Christmas tree," they answered. "Christ always has a Christmas tree on this day, for the little children who have no tree of their own...." And he found out that all these little boys and girls were children just like himself; that some had been frozen in the baskets in which they had as babies been laid on the doorsteps of well-to-do Petersburg people, others had been boarded out with Finnish women by the Foundling and had been suffocated, others had died at their starved mother's breasts (in the Samara famine), others had died in the third-class railway carriages from the foul air; and yet they were all here, they were all like angels about Christ, and He was in the midst of them and held out His hands to them and blessed them and their sinful mothers.... And the mothers of these children stood on one side weeping; each one knew her boy or girl, and the children flew up to them and kissed them and wiped away their tears with their little hands, and begged them not to weep because they were so happy.

And down below in the morning, the porter found the little dead body of the frozen child on the wood stack; they sought out his mother too.... She had died before him. They met before the Lord God in heaven.

Why have I made up such a story, so out of keeping with an ordinary diary, and a writer's above all? And I promised two stories dealing with real events! But that is just it, I keep fancying that all this may have happened really—that is, what took place in the cellar and on the wood stack; but as for Christ's Christmas tree, I cannot tell you whether that could have happened or not.

Scribbling Notes

CHAPTER XVII

To My Little Girl

To My Little Girl

Zofia Romanowicz

    I'll make a set of dishes for my little girl,
I think it will be lovely;
I'll mold goblets,
I'll turn plates,
I'll paint it with wonders,
Suns, stars, birds –
How my little girl will clap her hands!
    But if her little hand thoughtlessly
Bumps something and the set shatters,
Don't cry, my little one.
Our life too is fragile!
More fragile than these goblets
With their painted stars –
Do you know – my heart is full of bloody shards . . .
    Scribbling Notes

CHAPTER XVIII

Mushrooms in the city

Mushrooms in the city

Italo Calvino

The wind, coming to the city from far away, brings it unusual gifts, noticed by only a few sensitive souls, such as hay-fever victims, who sneeze at the pollen from flowers of other lands.

One day, to the narrow strip of ground flanking a city avenue came a gust of spores from God knows where; and some mushrooms germinated. Nobody noticed them except
Marcovaldo, the worker who caught his tram just there every morning.

This Marcovaldo possessed an eye ill-suited to city life: billboards, traffic-lights, shop-windows, neon signs, posters,
no matter how carefully devised to catch the attention, never arrested his gaze, which might have been running over the desert sands. Instead, he would never miss a leaf yellowing on a branch, a feather trapped by a roof-tile; there was no horsefly on a horse's back, no worm-hole in a plank, or fig-peel squashed on the sidewalk that Marcovaldo
didn't remark and ponder over, discovering the changes of season, the yearnings of his heart, and the woes of his existence.

Thus, one morning, as he was waiting for the tram that would take him to Sbav and Co., where he was employed as an unskilled laborer, he noticed something unusual near the stop, in the sterile, encrusted strip of earth beneath the

avenue's line of trees; at certain points, near the tree trunks,
some bumps seemed to rise and, here and there, they had opened, allowing roundish subterranean bodies to peep out,

Bending to tie his shoes, he took a better look: they were mushrooms, real mushrooms, sprouting right in the heart of the city! To Marcovaldo the gray and wretched world surrounding him seemed suddenly generous with hidden riches; something could still be expected of life, beyond the hourly wage of his stipulated salary, with inflation index, family grant, and cost-of-living allowance,

On the job he was more absent-minded than usual; he kept thinking that while he was there unloading cases and boxes, in the darkness of the earth the slow, silent mush-rooms, known only to him, were ripening their porous flesh, were assimilating underground humors, breaking the crust of clods. "One night's rain would be enough," he said to himself, "then they would be ready to pick." And he

couldn't wait to share his discovery with his wife and his six
children.

"T'm telling you!" he announced during their scant supper.

"In a week's time we'll be eating mushrooms! A great fry!
That's a promise!"

And to the smaller children, who did not know what mushrooms were, he explained ecstatically the beauty of

the numerous species, the delicacy of their flavor, the way
they should be cooked; and so he also drew into the dis-
cussion his wife, Domitilla, who until then had appeared
rather incredulous and abstracted,

"Where are these mushrooms?" the children asked.
"Tell
us where they grow!"

At this question Marcovaldo's enthusiasm was curbed
by
a suspicious thought: Now ifI tell them the place, they'll go
and hunt for them with the usual gang of kids, word will
spread through the neighborhood, and the mushrooms will
end up in somebody else's pan! And so that discovery,
which had promptly filled his heart with universal love,

now made him wildly possessive, surrounded him with
Jealous and distrusting fear.

"I know where the mushrooms are, and I'm the only one
who knows," he said to his children, 'and God help you if
you breathe a word to anybody."

The next morning, as he approached the tram stop,
Marcovaldo was filled with apprehension. He bent to look
at the ground and, to his relief, saw that the mushrooms had
grown a little, but not much, and were still almost
completely hidden by the earth.

He was bent in this position when he realized there was
someone behind him. He straightened up at once and tried
to act indifferent. It was the street-cleaner, leaning on his
broom and looking at him.

This street-cleaner, whose jurisdiction included the
place
where the mushrooms grew, was a lanky youth with eye-
glasses. His name was Amadigi, and Marcovaldo had long
harbored a dislike of him, perhaps because of those eye-

glasses that examined the pavement of the streets, seeking any trace of nature, to be eradicated by his broom,

It was Saturday; and Marcovaldo spent his free half-day circling the bed of dirt with an absent air, keeping an eye on the street-cleaner in the distance and on the mushrooms, and calculating how much time they needed to ripen.

That night it rained: like peasants who, after months of drought, wake up and leap with joy at the sound of the first drops, so Marcovaldo, alone in all the city, sat up in bed and called to his family: "It's raining! It's raining!" and breathed in the smell of moistened dust and fresh mold that came from outside.

At dawn — it was Sunday ~ with the children and a borrowed basket, he ran immediately to the patch. There were the mushrooms, erect on their stems, their caps high over the still-soaked earth. "Hurrah!" — and they fell to gathering them.

"Papa! Look how many that man over there has found," Michelino said, and his father, raising his eyes, saw Amadigi standing beside them, also with a basket full of mushrooms
under his arm,

"Ah, you're gathering them, too?" the street-cleaner said.
"Then they're edible? I picked a few, but I wasn't sure . . . Farther down the avenue some others have sprouted, even bigger ones . . . Well, now that I know, I'll tell my relatives; they're down there arguing whether it's a good idea to pick them or not. . ." And he walked off in a hurry.

Marcovaldo was speechless: even bigger mushrooms, which he hadn't noticed, an unhoped-for harvest, being taken from him like this, before his very eyes. For amoment he was almost frozen with anger, fury, then — as sometimes

happens — the collapse of individual passion led to a generous
impulse. At that hour, many people were waiting for the
tram, umbrellas over their arms, because the weather was
still damp and uncertain. "Hey, you! Do you want to eat
fried mushrooms tonight?" Marcovaldo shouted to the
crowd of people at the stop. "Mushrooms are growing here
by the street! Come along! There's plenty for all!" And he
walked off after Amadigi, with a string of people behind
him.

They all found plenty of mushrooms, and lacking baskets,
they used their open umbrellas. Somebody said: "It would
be nice to have a big feast, all of us together!" But, instead,
each took his own share and went home.

They saw one another again soon, however; that very
evening, in fact, in the same ward of the hospital, after the
stomach-pump had saved them all from poisoning. It was
not serious, because the number of mushrooms eaten by
each person was quite small.

Marcovaldo and Amadigi had adjacent beds; they glared
at each other.

Scribbling Notes

CHAPTER XIX

Yellow Brick Road by Witi Ihimaera

Yellow Brick Road

by Witi Ihimaera
   Follow the yellow brick road,
Follow, follow, follow follow,
Follow the yellow brick road ...
We're almost there! Almost at Wellington, the Emerald
City! Me and Dad and Mum and Roha, we been
travelling for two days now in our car which Dad bought
from Mr Wallace last week. No dents and honk honk
goes the horn. Dad, he said I could have a drive of it myself
when we left Waituhi but then it conked out on the
Whareratas and that made him change his mind.
- I told you we wouldn't get to Wellington in this, Mum said
to him while he was fixing it up.
- We'll get there.
- But I want to get there in one piece! Mum answered.
- Throw some of your junk out then, Dad told her.
Our car sure is loaded down all right. Mum's stuff is in the
boot, some belongings are tied under the
canvas on the roof and there's even some squeezed in here
with us. Boy.
But you won't conk out now, ay car? There's just one hill to
go and we'll be there. So up we go, up the
hill, slowly but surely. And who cares if cars bank up
behind us! They can beep all they like. We got as much
right to be on this road as they got.

Road, road, yellow brick road, yellow with the headlights sweeping across it. Just like in that book Miss
Wright, my teacher, gave me before we left Waituhi. A neat book. About the straw man, the tin man, the
cowardly lion and the Emerald City and ... we're almost there!
I bounce up and down on the seat. I can't wait to see all the sparkling green towers glittering in the dark
ahead of us.
- Matiu, you just sit still! Mum growls. What's gotten into you,
ay?
- Sorry, Mum.
Poor Mum. She's very tired and still unhappy about leaving Waituhi, our whanau, our family. Her eyes
are still red with the crying when all the people had waved goodbye to us like little flags fluttering far away. At
least she hasn't cried as often as Roha has for Hone though! Roha and Hone, they went round together and
once I saw them having a pash. Eeee!
I grin at my big sister. Never mind, Roha. Plenty other boys down.inWellington and you can pash up
large with them when we get there, ay.
- What you grinning for, Smarty? Roha snaps.
- I'm allowed to grin if I want to, aren't I? I ask, suddenly hurt.
- All right, all right, you don't have to scream.
I make a funny face at her. It would teach her a good lesson if even the pakehas didn't want to pash with
her! Lots of pakehas in Wellington. Not like in Waituhi. Makes me scared to think about it.
- Dad, will the pakehas like us in Wellington? Dad?
He doesn't answer me because he is driving carefully. He

has to lean forward to see the road in front of
him. It has started to rain.
Wish I was older and knew how to drive better. Then I
could give him a rest at the wheel.
I press against him and he puts an arm round me. His face
looks tired, just like it looked when we were
walking to a garage yesterday after our car ran out of petrol.
There we were, miles from anywhere, walking along
the road while car after car sped past us without stopping.
Some of them blared loudly at us. Others made a lot
of dust come over us. And always as they passed the faces
would be looking back and staring at us. I felt
puzzled.
- Why don't they stop, Dad?
He had shrugged his shoulders.
- We're in a different country now, son.
I began to hate those faces. I wanted to throw stones at
them all. But things will be different when we
get to Wellington, won't the? And we will be happy, won't
we?
Course we will. You just wait and see, Dad. We'll make lots
of money and be rich as anything because
Wellington is where the money is. And you have to go
where the money is, ay Dad. No use staying in Waituhi
and being poor all the time, ay.

I lean back in the seat and burrow under the blanket. It is
getting cold and there is a draught coming
through a hole in our car. I feel my bag of lollies in my
pocket.
- You want one, Mum? You want one, Dad? Roha?
I pass the bag to Roha and she takes two, the greedy thing.
I put one in my mouth and count what's left.

Seven.
Boy, these are the dearest lollies I ever bought. When we stopped at the shop yesterday I gave the man
thirty cents and he didn't give me any change. When I asked him for it, he told me thirty cents was how much
these lollies cost. But he was lying. He was a thief and he stole my money. How would he like it if someone
rooked him'? What's more, these lollies stink, just like him.
I watch the road as it twists ahead through the dark. Every now and then, there is a loud whoosh of a
fast car passing us. Those fast cars don't like us. We're too slow for them.
Suddenly, I see two lights ahead like eyes glaring at us. The eyes open wider, grow larger, looking like the
eyes of a...
- Dad! I yell, afraid.
A big truck descends on us with its headlight blazing full. I seem to see taloned fingers reaching out to
claw me.
- Bloody hell, Dad mutters.
He swerves. The car kicks gravel. The truck thunders past, screaming in the wind.
I look at Mum. Her face is shaken.
- I better keep both my hands on the wheel, Dad says.
He lifts his arm from me and I feel suddenly alone. I begin to think of Waituhi, our whanau, and that
makes me sad. All our family was there and Emere was our cow. Haere ra, Emere. And haere ra to you, e Hemi.
You'll always be my best mate.
I start humming to myself. Quietly.
- Follow the yellow brick road,
Follow follow, follow, follow...
Miss Wright, she taught us that song at school. A neat song.

We made a long line, joined by our hands,
and danced crazy patterns over the playground and...
There is a snapping sound and the flapping of canvas. -
What's that, Dad?
He pulls the car over to the side of the road and steps out.
Mum winds down her window.
- What's wrong?
- Rope's snapped, he yells back.
- You better get out and help your father, Mum says to me.
I jump out into the rain. Boy, it's sure wet and cold out here.
Dad is struggling in the wind to pull the
canvas back over our belongings.
- All this junk! Dad mutters. No wonder the canvas came
away. He takes a box from the top and dumps
it on the side of the road. My books spill out and the pages
fly away like birds in the wind.
- Dad. No, Dad...
I run out into the road in panic because those are my school
books and among them is my best book.
My best book.
- Matiu! Get off the road! Mum screams.
My best book. In the wind and the rain. My best book.
- Matiu.
And there it is. Lying there on the road. I run to get it and
car brakes scream in my ears.
But I have it in my arms and hold it safe to me. And I don't
care if I get a hiding. I don't care...
Mum hits me very hard.
-What you want to do that for, you stupid kid.
But I don't care. I don't care...
And the driver of the other car is saying angry words to
Dad:
- What the bloody hell do you think you're up to, eh'?

Letting your kid run out like that, what's wrong
with you! Look, never mind about bloody arguing. Christ,
you shouldn't be on the road at all. Your car's bloody
dangerous loaded like that. And why the hell didn't you pull
further off the road, eh? Oh, what's the use. You
Maoris are all the same. Dumb bloody horis.
He steps back into his car and roars off. Dad comes towards
me and his face is full of anger.
Go ahead, Dad. Hit me. I deserve it.

But he doesn't. Instead, he hugs me and asks:
- You all right, son?
- Yes, Dad. I'm sorry, Dad. That man...
- That bastard. Never mind about him.
I clutch my book tightly. I carry it into the car with me.
Mum starts to get angry with me again.
Tuni tuni, woman, Dad says. It's all over now. Let's forget it.
- It wouldn't have happened if you'd tied down our things
properly like Sam told you to do, Mum
answers.
Sam is my uncle and we stayed at his place in Hastings last
night. Uncle Sam didn't even know we were
on our way to Wellington.
- Down to that windy place" he'd said. You fullas better tie
yourselves down or you'll be blown away!
Don't you know how cold it is down there'? Brother, it's
liquid sunshine all the year round!
- We don't care, I'd answered him. We're going to make lots
of money down there. Not much room left
for pa living anymore. That's what you said, ay Dad.
Dad had looked at me strangely.
- No more jobs back home, he told Uncle. Plenty of the
seasonal work, yes, but me and Hine had

enough of that. We had enough of shearing, the fruit-picking and the going down South to shear some more.
No, plenty of work in Wellington. Plenty of factories.
- Who told you that! Uncle snorted.
- Jim, Dad answered.
Uncle Jim is Dad's brother. He lives in Petone and we're going to stay with him until we find our own
house.
Uncle Sam had shrugged his shoulders..
- Well, Jim should know, he'd said.
- I want us to have a good life, a new start, Dad tried to explain. A new start for my kids. Me and Hine,
we've always had nothing. But my kids? They're going to grow up with everything. I'll fight for it, because they
must have it.
But I'd seen Uncle Sam hadn't understood Dad's words. He'd simply shaken his head and wished us
luck. And in the morning before we left he'd told Dad to tie the canvas down tight.
- Otherwise that wind will get under it and before you know it you'll be flying into Wellington!
Dad had tried his best with the ropes. He'd said to Mum:
- How about getting rid of some of this junk, ay?
She'd answered him:
- This junk is all we've ever had. I'm not throwing away one piece of it, wind or no wind.
It sure is windy all right, outside the car. The clouds are rushing in the night sky just like the Winged
Monkeys. The wind moans and chatters and cackles among our belongings, and I must close my eyes and put
my hands to my ears to shut out the sights and sounds of this night.
Then, suddenly, all the noises stop. Even the car has

stopped.

- There it is, Dad says.

I open my eyes. Far away are the lights of Wellington, streaming

with the rain down our window like glistening towers. And it looks so... so... beautiful. Just as I'd imagined it to

be. Just as I'd pretended it would be. Emerald City.

- Isn't it neat, Muni'?

She stares ahead. Her face is still. - Roha? I ask.

My sister's face is filled with a strange glow.

- Dad?

He looks at me and smiles.

- You and your dreams, son.

He starts the car. We begin to drive down from the hill. I look at Dad and Mum and Roha, puzzled.

How come I'm the only one to be happy!

Can't they see this is where our life begins and this is where our dreams begin'?

And dreams, they come true, don't they? Don't they?

I look out the car. I see the sign: STEEP GRADE. All along the yellow brick road there have been signs

like that. STEEP GRADE. CHANGE DOWN. ONE WAY. LIMITED SPEED ZONE. ROAD NARROWS.

STOP. WINDING ROAD. GO. CONCEALED EXIT

TRAFFIC LIGHTS AHEAD. GREASY WHEN WET. NO EXIT. NO PASSING. NO STOPPING.

Many signs, all telling us where we have to go and.... I begin to feel scared.

If ever we want to, will we be able to find our way back'?

I begin to sing to myself. Not because I'm happy, but because I think I want to feel sure myself

everything will turn out alright.

It will, won't it?
Follow the yellow brick road,
Follow, follow, follow, follow,
Follow...
    Scribbling Notes

CHAPTER XX

Last Contact

Last Contact

=Stephen Baxter

March 15th

Caitlin walked into the garden through the little gate from the drive. Maureen was working on the lawn.

Just at that moment Maureen's phone pinged. She took off her gardening gloves, dug the phone out of the deep pocket of her old quilted coat and looked at the screen. "Another contact," she called to her daughter.

Caitlin looked cold in her thin jacket; she wrapped her arms around her body. "Another super-civilization discovered, off in space. We live in strange times, Mum."

"That's the fifteenth this year. And I did my bit to help discover it. Good for me," Maureen said, smiling. "Hello, love." She leaned forward for a kiss on the cheek.

She knew why Caitlin was here, of course. Caitlin had always hinted she would come and deliver the news about the Big Rip in person, one way or the other. Maureen guessed what that news was from her daughter's hollow, stressed eyes. But Caitlin was looking around the garden, and Maureen decided to let her tell it all in her own time.

She asked, "How're the kids?"

"Fine. At school. Bill's at home, baking bread." Caitlin smiled. "Why do stay-at-home fathers always bake bread? But he's starting at Webster's next month."

"That's the engineers in Oxford?"

"That's right. Not that it makes much difference now. We won't run out of money before, well, before it doesn't matter." Caitlin considered the garden. It was just a scrap of lawn really, with a quite nicely stocked border, behind a cottage that was a little more than a hundred years old, in this village on the outskirts of Oxford. "It's the first time I've seen this properly."

"Well, it's the first bright day we've had. My first spring here." They walked around the lawn. "It's not bad. It's been let to run to seed a bit by Mrs. Murdoch. Who was another lonely old widow," Maureen said.

"You mustn't think like that."

"Well, it's true. This little house is fine for someone on their own, like me, or her. I suppose I'd pass it on to somebody else in the same boat, when I'm done."

Caitlin was silent at that, silent at the mention of the future.

Maureen showed her patches where the lawn had dried out last summer and would need reseeding. And there was a little brass plaque fixed to the wall of the house to show the level reached by the Thames floods of two years ago. "The lawn is all right. I do like this time of year when you sort of wake it up from the winter. The grass needs raking and scarifying, of course. I'll reseed bits of it, and see how it grows during the summer. I might think about getting some of it relaid. Now the weather's so different, the drainage might not be right anymore."

"You're enjoying getting back in the saddle, aren't you, Mum?"

Maureen shrugged. "Well, the last couple of years weren't much fun. Nursing your dad, and then getting rid of the house. It's nice to get this old thing back on again." She raised her arms and looked down at her quilted gardening coat.

Caitlin wrinkled her nose. "I always hated that stupid old coat. You really should get yourself something better, Mum. These modern fabrics are very good."

"This will see me out," Maureen said firmly.

They walked around the verge, looking at the plants, the weeds, the autumn leaves that hadn't been swept up and were now rotting in place.

Caitlin said, "I'm going to be on the radio later. BBC Radio 4. There's to be a government statement on the Rip, and I'll be in the follow-up discussion. It starts at nine, and I should be on about nine-thirty."

"I'll listen to it. Do you want me to tape it for you?"

"No. Bill will get it. Besides, you can listen to all these things on the websites these days."

Maureen said carefully, "I take it the news is what you expected, then."

"Pretty much. The Hawaii observatories confirmed it. I've seen the new Hubble images, deep sky fields. Empty, save for the foreground objects. All the galaxies beyond the local group have gone. Eerie, really, seeing your predictions come true like that. That's couch grass, isn't it?"

"Yes. I stuck a fork in it. Nothing but root mass underneath. It will be a devil to get up. I'll have a go, and then put down some bin liners for a few weeks, and see if that kills it off. Then there are these roses that should have been pruned by now. I think I'll plant some gladioli in this corner—"

"Mum, it's October." Caitlin blurted that out. She looked thin, pale, and tense, a real office worker, but then Maureen had always thought that about her daughter, that she worked too hard. Now she was thirty-five, and her moderately pretty face was lined at the eyes and around her mouth, the first wistful signs of age. "October 14th, at about four in the afternoon. I say 'about.' I could give you the time down to the attosecond if you wanted."

Maureen took her hands. "It's all right, love. It's about when you thought it would be, isn't it?"

"Not that it does us any good, knowing. There's nothing we can do about it."

They walked on. They came to a corner on the south side of the little garden. "This ought to catch the sun," Maureen said. "I'm thinking of putting in a seat here. A pergola maybe. Somewhere to sit. I'll see how the sun goes around later in the year."

"Dad would have liked a pergola," Caitlin said. "He always did say a garden was a place to sit in, not to work."

"Yes. It does feel odd that your father died, so soon before all this. I'd have liked him to see it out. It seems a waste somehow."

Caitlin looked up at the sky. "Funny thing, Mum. It's all quite invisible to the naked eye still. You can see the Andromeda Galaxy, just, but that's bound to the Milky Way by gravity. So the expansion hasn't reached down to the scale of the visible, not yet. It's still all instruments, telescopes. But it's real all right."

"I suppose you'll have to explain it all on Radio 4."

"That's why I'm there. We'll probably have to keep saying it over and over, trying to find ways of saying it that people can understand. You know, don't you, Mum? It's all to do with dark energy. It's like an antigravity field that permeates the universe. Just as gravity pulls everything together, the dark energy is pulling the universe apart, taking more and more of it so far away that its light can't reach us anymore. It started at the level of the largest structures in the universe, superclusters of galaxies. But in the end it will fold down to the smallest scales. Every bound structure will be pulled apart. Even atoms, even subatomic particles. The Big Rip.

"We've known about this stuff for years. What we didn't expect was that the expansion would accelerate as it has. We thought we had trillions of years. Then the forecast was billions. And now—"

"Yes."

"It's funny for me being involved in this stuff, Mum. Being on the radio. I've never been a people person. I became an astrophysicist, for God's sake. I always thought that what I studied would have absolutely no effect on anybody's life. How wrong I was. Actually there's been a lot of debate about whether to announce it or not."

"I think people will behave pretty well," Maureen said. "They usually do. It might get trickier toward the end, I suppose. But people have a right to know, don't you think?"

"They're putting it on after nine, so people can decide what to tell their kids."

"After the watershed! Well, that's considerate. Will you tell your two?"

"I think we'll have to. Everybody at school will know. They'll probably get bullied about it if they don't know. Imagine that. Besides, the little beggars will probably have googled it on their mobiles by one minute past nine."

Maureen laughed. "There is that."

"It will be like when I told them Dad had died," Caitlin said. "Or like when Billy started asking hard questions about Santa Claus."

"No more Christmases," Maureen said suddenly. "If it's all over in October."

"No more birthdays for my two either," Caitlin said.

"November and January."

"Yes. It's funny, in the lab, when the date came up, that was the first thing I thought of."

Maureen's phone pinged again. "Another signal. Quite different in nature from the last, according to this."

"I wonder if we'll get any of those signals decoded in time."

Maureen waggled her phone. "It won't be for want of trying, me and a billion other search-for-ET-at-home enthusiasts. Would you like some tea, love?"

"It's all right. I'll let you get on. I told Bill I'd get the shopping in, before I have to go back to the studios in Oxford this evening."

They walked toward the back door into the house, strolling, inspecting the plants and the scrappy lawn.

June 5th

It was about lunchtime when Caitlin arrived from the garden center with the pieces of the pergola. Maureen helped her unload them from the back of a white van, and carry them through the gate from the drive. They were mostly just prefabricated wooden panels and beams that they could manage between the two of them, though the big iron spikes that would be driven into the ground to support the uprights were heavier. They got the pieces stacked upon the lawn.

"I should be able to set it up myself," Maureen said. "Joe next door said he'd lay the concrete base for me, and help me lift on the roof section. There's some nailing to be done, and creosoting, but I can do all that."

"Joe, eh?" Caitlin grinned.

"Oh, shut up, he's just a neighbor. Where did you get the van? Did you have to hire it?"

"No, the garden center loaned it to me. They can't deliver. They are still getting stock in, but they can't rely on the staff.

They just quit, without any notice. In the end it sort of gets to you, I suppose."

"Well, you can't blame people for wanting to be at home."

"No. Actually Bill's packed it in. I meant to tell you. He didn't even finish his induction at Webster's. But the project he was working on would never have got finished anyway."

"I'm sure the kids are glad to have him home."

"Well, they're finishing the school year. At least I think they will, the teachers still seem keen to carry on."

"It's probably best for them."

"Yes. We can always decide what to do after the summer, if the schools open again."

Maureen had prepared some sandwiches, and some iced elderflower cordial. They sat in the shade of the house and ate their lunch and looked out over the garden.

Caitlin said, "Your lawn's looking good."

"It's come up quite well. I'm still thinking of relaying that patch over there."

"And you put in a lot of vegetables in the end," Caitlin said.

"I thought I should. I've planted courgettes and French beans and carrots, and a few outdoor tomatoes. I could do with a greenhouse, but I haven't really room for one. It seemed a good idea, rather than flowers, this year."

"Yes. You can't rely on the shops."

Things had kept working, mostly, as people stuck to their jobs. But there were always gaps on the supermarket shelves, as supply chains broke down. There was talk of rationing some essentials, and there were already coupons for petrol.

"I don't approve of how tatty the streets are getting in town," Maureen said sternly.

Caitlin sighed. "I suppose you can't blame people for packing in a job like street-sweeping. It is a bit tricky getting around town though. We need some work done on the roof, we're missing a couple of tiles. It's just as well we won't have to get through another winter," she said, a bit darkly. "But you can't get a builder for love or money."

"Well, you never could."

They both laughed.

Maureen said, "I told you people would cope. People do just get on with things."

"We haven't got to the end game yet," Caitlin said. "I went into London the other day. That isn't too friendly, Mum. It's not all like this, you know."

Maureen's phone pinged, and she checked the screen. "Four or five a day now," she said. "New contacts, lighting up all over the sky."

"But that's down from the peak, isn't it?"

"Oh, we had a dozen a day at one time. But now we've lost half the stars, haven't we?"

"Well, that's true, now the Rip has folded down into the galaxy. I haven't really been following it, Mum. Nobody's been able to decode any of the signals, have they?"

"But some of them aren't the sort of signal you can decode anyhow. In one case somebody picked up an artificial element in the spectrum of a star. Something that was manufactured, and then just chucked in to burn up, like a flare."

Caitlin considered. "That can't say anything but 'here we are,' I suppose."

"Maybe that's enough."

"Yes."

It had really been Harry who had been interested in wild speculations about alien life and so forth. Joining the phone network of home observers of ET, helping to analyze possible signals from the stars in a network of millions of others, had been Harry's hobby, not Maureen's. It was one of Harry's things she had kept up after he had died, like his weather monitoring and his football pools. It would have felt odd just to have stopped it all.

But she did understand how remarkable it was that the sky had suddenly lit up with messages like a Christmas tree, after more than half a century of dogged, fruitless, frustrating listening. Harry would have loved to see it.

"Caitlin, I don't really understand how all these signals can be arriving just now. I mean, it takes years for light to travel between the stars, doesn't it? We only knew about the phantom energy a few months ago."

"But others might have detected it long before, with better technology than we've got. That would give you time to send something. Maybe the signals have been timed to get here, just before the end, aimed just at us."

"That's a nice thought."

"Some of us hoped that there would be an answer to the dark energy in all those messages."

"What answer could there be?"

Caitlin shrugged. "If we can't decode the messages we'll never know. And I suppose if there was anything to be done, it would have been done by now."

"I don't think the messages need decoding," Maureen said.

Caitlin looked at her curiously, but didn't pursue it. "Listen, Mum. Some of us are going to try to do something. You understand that the Rip works down the scales, so that larger structures break up first. The galaxy, then the solar system, then planets like Earth. And then the human body."

Maureen considered. "So people will outlive the Earth."

"Well, they could. For maybe about thirty minutes, until atomic structures get pulled apart. There's talk of establishing a sort of shelter in Oxford that could survive the end of the Earth. Like a submarine, I suppose. And if you wore a pressure suit you might last a bit longer even than that. The design goal is to make it through to the last microsecond. You could gather another thirty minutes of data that way. They've asked me to go in there."

"Will you?"

"I haven't decided. It will depend on how we feel about the kids, and—you know."

Maureen considered. "You must do what makes you happy, I suppose."

"Yes. But it's hard to know what that is, isn't it?" Caitlin looked up at the sky. "It's going to be a hot day."

"Yes. And a long one. I think I'm glad about that. The night sky looks odd now the Milky Way has gone."

"And the stars are flying off one by one," Caitlin murmured. "I suppose the constellations will look funny by the autumn."

"Do you want some more sandwiches?"

"I'll have a bit more of that cordial. It's very good, Mum."

"It's elderflower. I collect the blossoms from that bush down the road. I'll give you the recipe if you like."

"Shall we see if your Joe fancies laying a bit of concrete this afternoon? I could do with meeting your new beau."

"Oh, shut up," Maureen said, and she went inside to make a fresh jug of cordial.

October 14th

That morning Maureen got up early. She was pleased that it was a bright morning, after the rain of the last few days. It was a lovely autumn day. She had breakfast listening to the last-ever episode of The Archers, but her radio battery failed before the end.

She went to work in the garden, hoping to get everything done before the light went. There was plenty of work, leaves to rake up, the roses and the clematis to prune. She had decided to plant a row of daffodil bulbs around the base of the new pergola. She noticed a little band of goldfinches, plundering a clump of Michaelmas daisies for seed. She sat back on her heels to watch. The colorful little birds had always been her favorites.

Then the light went, just like that, darkening as if somebody was throwing a dimmer switch. Maureen looked up. The sun was rushing away, and sucking all the light out of the sky with it. It was a remarkable sight, and she wished she had a camera. As the light turned gray, and then charcoal, and then utterly black, she heard the goldfinches fly off in a clatter, confused. It had only taken a few minutes.

Maureen was prepared. She dug a little torch out of the pocket of her old quilted coat. She had been hoarding the batteries; you hadn't been able to buy them for weeks. The torch got her as far as the pergola, where she lit some rush torches that she'd fixed to canes.

Then she sat in the pergola, in the dark, with her garden lit up by her rush torches, and waited. She wished she had thought to bring out her book. She didn't suppose there would be time to finish it now. Anyhow, the flickering firelight would be bad for her eyes.

"Mum?"

The soft voice made her jump. It was Caitlin, threading her way across the garden with a torch of her own.

"I'm in here, love."

Caitlin joined her mother in the pergola, and they sat on the wooden benches, on the thin cushions Maureen had been able to buy. Caitlin shut down her torch to conserve the battery.

Maureen said, "The sun went, right on cue."

"Oh, it's all working out, bang on time."

Somewhere there was shouting, whooping, a tinkle of broken glass.

"Someone's having fun," Maureen said.

"It's a bit like an eclipse," Caitlin said. "Like in Cornwall, do you remember? The sky was cloudy, and we couldn't see a bit of the eclipse. But at that moment when the sky went dark, everybody got excited. Something primeval, I suppose."

"Would you like a drink? I've got a flask of tea. The milk's a bit off, I'm afraid."

"I'm fine, thanks."

"I got up early and managed to get my bulbs in. I didn't have time to trim that clematis, though. I got it all ready for the winter, I think."

"I'm glad."

"I'd rather be out here than indoors, wouldn't you?"

"Oh, yes."

"I thought about bringing blankets. I didn't know if it would get cold."

"Not much. The air will keep its heat for a bit. There won't be time to get very cold."

"I was going to fix up some electric lights out here. But the power's been off for days."

"The rushes are better, anyway. I would have been here earlier. There was a jam by the church. All the churches are packed, I imagine. And then I ran out of petrol a couple of miles back. We haven't been able to fill up for weeks."

"It's all right. I'm glad to see you. I didn't expect you at all. I couldn't ring." Even the phone networks had been down for days. In the end everything had slowly broken down, as people simply gave up their jobs and went home. Maureen asked carefully, "So how's Bill and the kids?"

"We had an early Christmas," Caitlin said. "They'll both miss their birthdays, but we didn't think they should be cheated out of Christmas too. We did it all this morning. Stockings, a tree, the decorations and the lights down from the loft, presents, the lot. And then we had a big lunch. I couldn't find a turkey but I'd been saving a chicken. After lunch the kids went for their nap. Bill put their pills in their lemonade."

Maureen knew she meant the little blue pills the NHS had given out to every household.

"Bill lay down with them. He said he was going to wait with them until he was sure—you know. That they wouldn't wake up, and be distressed. Then he was going to take his own pill."

Maureen took her hand. "You didn't stay with them?"

"I didn't want to take the pill." There was some bitterness in her voice. "I always wanted to see it through to the end. I suppose it's the scientist in me. We argued about it. We fought, I suppose. In the end we decided this way was the best."

Maureen thought that on some level Caitlin couldn't really believe her children were gone, or she couldn't keep functioning like this. "Well, I'm glad you're here with me. And I never fancied those pills either. Although—will it hurt?"

"Only briefly. When the Earth's crust gives way. It will be like sitting on top of an erupting volcano."

"You had an early Christmas. Now we're going to have an early Bonfire Night."

"It looks like it. I wanted to see it through," Caitlin said again. "After all I was in at the start—those supernova studies."

"You mustn't think it's somehow your fault."

"I do, a bit," Caitlin confessed. "Stupid, isn't it?"

"But you decided not to go to the shelter in Oxford with the others?"

"I'd rather be here. With you. Oh, but I brought this." She dug into her coat pocket and produced a sphere, about the size of a tennis ball.

Maureen took it. It was heavy, with a smooth black surface.

Caitlin said, "It's the stuff they make space shuttle heatshield tiles out of. It can soak up a lot of heat."

"So it will survive the Earth breaking up."

"That's the idea."

"Are there instruments inside?"

"Yes. It should keep working, keep recording until the expansion gets down to the centimeter scale, and the Rip cracks the sphere open. Then it will release a cloud of even finer sensor units, motes we call them. It's nanotechnology, Mum, machines the size of molecules. They will keep gathering data until the expansion reaches molecular scales."

"How long will that take after the big sphere breaks up?"

"Oh, a microsecond or so. There's nothing we could come up with that could keep data-gathering after that."

Maureen hefted the little device. "What a wonderful little gadget. It's a shame nobody will be able to use its data."

"Well, you never know," Caitlin said. "Some of the cosmologists say this is just a transition, rather than an end. The universe has passed through transitions before, for instance from an age dominated by radiation to one dominated by matter—our age. Maybe there will be life of some kind in a new era dominated by the dark energy."

"But nothing like us."

"I'm afraid not."

Maureen stood and put the sphere down in the middle of the lawn. The grass was just faintly moist, with dew, as the air cooled.

"Will it be all right here?"

"I should think so."

The ground shuddered, and there was a sound like a door slamming, deep in the ground. Alarms went off, from cars and houses, distant wails. Maureen hurried back to the pergola. She sat with Caitlin, and they wrapped their arms around each other. Caitlin raised her wrist to peer at her watch, then gave it up. "I don't suppose we need a countdown."

The ground shook more violently, and there was an odd sound, like waves rushing over pebbles on a beach. Maureen peered out of the pergola. Remarkably, one wall of her house had given way, just like that, and the bricks had tumbled into a heap.

"You'll never get a builder out now," Caitlin said, but her voice was edgy.

"We'd better get out of here."

"All right."

They got out of the pergola and stood side by side on the lawn, over the little sphere of instruments, holding onto each other. There was another tremor, and Maureen's roof tiles slid to the ground, smashing and tinkling.

"Mum, there's one thing."

"Yes, love."

"You said you didn't think all those alien signals needed to be decoded."

"Why, no. I always thought it was obvious what all the signals were saying."

"What?"

Maureen tried to reply.

The ground burst open. The scrap of dewy lawn flung itself into the air, and Maureen was thrown down, her face pressed against the grass. She glimpsed houses and trees and people, all flying in the air, underlit by a furnace-red glow from beneath.

But she was still holding Caitlin. Caitlin's eyes were squeezed tight shut. "Goodbye," Maureen yelled. "They were just saying goodbye." But she couldn't tell if Caitlin could hear.

CHAPTER XXI

THE TINKER'S WEDDING

THE TINKER'S WEDDING

-JM Synge

PERSONS

MICHAEL BYRNE, a tinker.
MARY BYRNE, an old woman, his mother.
SARAH CASEY, a young tinker woman.
A PRIEST.

ACT I.
SCENE: A Village roadside after nightfall. A fire of sticks is burning near the ditch a little to the right. Michael is working beside it. In the background, on the left, a sort of tent and ragged clothes drying on the hedge. On the right a chapel-gate.
SARAH CASEY
coming in on right, eagerly.—We'll see his reverence this place, Michael Byrne, and he passing backward to his house to-night.
MICHAEL
grimly.—That'll be a sacred and a sainted joy!
SARAH
sharply.—It'll be small joy for yourself if you aren't ready

with my wedding ring. (She goes over to him.) Is it near done this time, or what way is it at all?

MICHAEL

A poor way only, Sarah Casey, for it's the divil's job making a ring, and you'll be having my hands destroyed in a short while the way I'll not be able to make a tin can at all maybe at the dawn of day.

SARAH

sitting down beside him and throwing sticks on the fire.—If it's the divil's job, let you mind it, and leave your speeches that would choke a fool.

MICHAEL

slowly and glumly.—And it's you'll go talking of fools, Sarah Casey, when no man did ever hear a lying story even of your like unto this mortal day. You to be going beside me a great while, and rearing a lot of them, and then to be setting off with your talk of getting married, and your driving me to it, and I not asking it at all.

[Sarah turns her back to him and arranges something in the ditch.

MICHAEL

angrily.—Can't you speak a word when I'm asking what is it ails you since the moon did change?

SARAH

musingly.—I'm thinking there isn't anything ails me, Michael Byrne; but the spring-time is a queer time, and it's queer thoughts maybe I do think at whiles.

MICHAEL

It's hard set you'd be to think queerer than welcome, Sarah Casey; but what will you gain dragging me to the priest this night, I'm saying, when it's new thoughts you'll be thinking at the dawn of day?

SARAH

teasingly.—It's at the dawn of day I do be thinking I'd have a right to be going off to the rich tinkers do be travelling from Tibradden to the Tara Hill; for it'd be a fine life to be driving with young Jaunting Jim, where there wouldn't be any big hills to break the back of you, with walking up and walking down.

MICHAEL

with dismay.—It's the like of that you do be thinking!

SARAH

The like of that, Michael Byrne, when there is a bit of sun in it, and a kind air, and a great smell coming from the thorn-trees is above your head.

MICHAEL

looks at her for a moment with horror, and then hands her the ring.—Will that fit you now?

SARAH

trying it on.—It's making it tight you are, and the edges sharp on the tin.

MICHAEL

looking at it carefully.—It's the fat of your own finger, Sarah Casey; and isn't it a mad thing I'm saying again that you'd be asking marriage of me, or making a talk of going away from me, and you thriving and getting your good health by the grace of the Almighty God?

SARAH

giving it back to him.—Fix it now, and it'll do, if you're wary you don't squeeze it again.

MICHAEL

moodily, working again.—It's easy saying be wary; there's many things easy said, Sarah Casey, you'd wonder a fool even would be saying at all. (He starts violently.) The divil mend you, I'm scalded again!

SARAH

scornfully.—If you are, it's a clumsy man you are this night, Michael Byrne (raising her voice); and let you make haste now, or herself will be coming with the porter.

MICHAEL

defiantly, raising his voice.—Let me make haste? I'll be making haste maybe to hit you a great clout; for I'm thinking on the day I got you above at Rathvanna, and the way you began crying out and saying, "I'll go back to my ma," and I'm thinking on the way I came behind you that time, and hit you a great clout in the lug, and how quiet and easy it was you came along with me from that hour to this present day.

SARAH

standing up and throwing all her sticks into the fire.—And a big fool I was too, maybe; but we'll be seeing Jaunting Jim to-morrow in Ballinaclash, and he after getting a great price for his white foal in the horse-fair of Wicklow, the way it'll be a great sight to see him squandering his share of gold, and he with a grand eye for a fine horse, and a grand eye for a woman.

MICHAEL

working again with impatience.—The divil do him good with the two of them.

SARAH

kicking up the ashes with her foot.—Ah, he's a great lad, I'm telling you, and it's proud and happy I'll be to see him, and he the first one called me the Beauty of Ballinacree, a fine name for a woman.

MICHAEL

with contempt.—It's the like of that name they do be putting on the horses they have below racing in Arklow. It's easy pleased you are, Sarah Casey, easy pleased with a big word, or the liar speaks it.

SARAH

Liar!

MICHAEL

Liar, surely.

SARAH

indignantly.—Liar, is it? Didn't you ever hear tell of the peelers followed me ten miles along the Glen Malure, and they talking love to me in the dark night, or of the children you'll meet coming from school and they saying one to the other, "It's this day we seen Sarah Casey, the Beauty of Ballinacree, a great sight surely."

MICHAEL

God help the lot of them!

SARAH

It's yourself you'll be calling God to help, in two weeks or three, when you'll be waking up in the dark night and thinking you see me coming with the sun on me, and I driving a high cart with Jaunting Jim going behind. It's lonesome and cold you'll be feeling the ditch where you'll be lying down that night, I'm telling you, and you hearing the old woman making a great noise in her sleep, and the bats squeaking in the trees.

MICHAEL

Whist. I hear some one coming the road.

SARAH

looking out right.—It's some one coming forward from the doctor's door.

MICHAEL

It's often his reverence does be in there playing cards, or drinking a sup, or singing songs, until the dawn of day.

SARAH

It's a big boast of a man with a long step on him and a

trumpeting voice. It's his reverence surely; and if you have the ring done, it's a great bargain we'll make now and he after drinking his glass.

MICHAEL

going to her and giving her the ring.—There's your ring, Sarah Casey; but I'm thinking he'll walk by and not stop to speak with the like of us at all.

SARAH

tidying herself, in great excitement.—Let you be sitting here and keeping a great blaze, the way he can look on my face; and let you seem to be working, for it's great love the like of him have to talk of work.

MICHAEL

moodily, sitting down and beginning to work at a tin can.—Great love surely.

SARAH

eagerly.—Make a great blaze now, Michael Byrne.

[The priest comes in on right; she comes forward in front of him.

SARAH

in a very plausible voice.—Good evening, your reverence. It's a grand fine night, by the grace of God.

PRIEST

The Lord have mercy on us! What kind of a living woman is it that you are at all?

SARAH

It's Sarah Casey I am, your reverence, the Beauty of Ballinacree, and it's Michael Byrne is below in the ditch.

PRIEST

A holy pair, surely! Let you get out of my way.

[He tries to pass by.

SARAH

keeping in front of him.—We are wanting a little word with

your reverence.

PRIEST

I haven't a halfpenny at all. Leave the road I'm saying.

SARAH

It isn't a halfpenny we're asking, holy father; but we were thinking maybe we'd have a right to be getting married; and we were thinking it's yourself would marry us for not a halfpenny at all; for you're a kind man, your reverence, a kind man with the poor.

PRIEST

with astonishment.—Is it marry you for nothing at all?

SARAH

It is, your reverence; and we were thinking maybe you'd give us a little small bit of silver to pay for the ring.

PRIEST

loudly.—Let you hold your tongue; let you be quiet, Sarah Casey. I've no silver at all for the like of you; and if you want to be married, let you pay your pound. I'd do it for a pound only, and that's making it a sight cheaper than I'd make it for one of my own pairs is living here in the place.

SARAH

Where would the like of us get a pound, your reverence?

PRIEST

Wouldn't you easy get it with your selling asses, and making cans, and your stealing east and west in Wicklow and Wexford and the county Meath? (He tries to pass her.) Let you leave the road, and not be plaguing me more.

SARAH

pleadingly, taking money from her pocket.—Wouldn't you have a little mercy on us, your reverence? (Holding out money.) Wouldn't you marry us for a half a sovereign, and it a nice shiny one with a view on it of the living king's mamma?

PRIEST

If it's ten shillings you have, let you get ten more the same way, and I'll marry you then.

SARAH

whining.—It's two years we are getting that bit, your reverence, with our pence and our halfpence and an odd three-penny bit; and if you don't marry us now, himself and the old woman, who has a great drouth, will be drinking it to-morrow in the fair (she puts her apron to her eyes, half sobbing), and then I won't be married any time, and I'll be saying till I'm an old woman: "It's a cruel and a wicked thing to be bred poor."

PRIEST

turning up towards the fire.—Let you not be crying, Sarah Casey. It's a queer woman you are to be crying at the like of that, and you your whole life walking the roads.

SARAH

sobbing.—It's two years we are getting the gold, your reverence, and now you won't marry us for that bit, and we hard-working poor people do be making cans in the dark night, and blinding our eyes with the black smoke from the bits of twigs we do be burning.

[An old woman is heard singing tipsily on the left.

PRIEST

looking at the can Michael is making.—When will you have that can done, Michael Byrne?

MICHAEL

In a short space only, your reverence, for I'm putting the last dab of solder on the rim.

PRIEST

Let you get a crown along with the ten shillings and the gallon can, Sarah Casey, and I will wed you so.

MARY

suddenly shouting behind, tipsily.—Larry was a fine lad,
I'm saying; Larry was a fine lad, Sarah Casey—

MICHAEL

Whist, now, the two of you. There's my mother coming,
and she'd have us destroyed if she heard the like of that talk
the time she's been drinking her fill.

MARY

comes in singing

And when we asked him what way he'd die,
And he hanging unrepented,
"Begob," says Larry, "that's all in my eye,
By the clergy first invented."

SARAH

Give me the jug now, or you'll have it spilt in the ditch.

MARY

holding the jug with both her hands, in a stilted voice.—Let
you leave me easy, Sarah Casey. I won't spill it, I'm saying.
God help you; are you thinking it's frothing full to the brim
it is at this hour of the night, and I after carrying it in my
two hands a long step from Jemmy Neill's?

MICHAEL

anxiously.—Is there a sup left at all?

SARAH

looking into the jug.—A little small sup only I'm thinking.

MARY

sees the priest, and holds out jug towards him.—God save
your reverence. I'm after bringing down a smart drop; and
let you drink it up now, for it's a middling drouthy man you
are at all times, God forgive you, and this night is cruel dry.

[She tries to go towards him. Sarah holds her back.

PRIEST

waving her away.—Let you not be falling to the flames.
Keep off, I'm saying.

MARY

persuasively.—Let you not be shy of us, your reverence.
Aren't we all sinners, God help us! Drink a sup now, I'm
telling you; and we won't let on a word about it till the
Judgment Day.

[She takes up a tin mug, pours some porter into it, and
gives it to him.

MARY

singing, and holding the jug in her hand.

A lonesome ditch in Ballygan
The day you're beating a tenpenny can;
A lonesome bank in Ballyduff
The time . . .

[She breaks off. It's a bad, wicked song, Sarah Casey; and let
you put me down now in the ditch, and I won't sing it till
himself will be gone; for it's bad enough he is, I'm thinking,
without ourselves making him worse.

SARAH

putting her down, to the priest, half laughing.—Don't mind
her at all, your reverence. She's no shame the time she's a
drop taken; and if it was the Holy Father from Rome was
in it, she'd give him a little sup out of her mug, and say the
same as she'd say to yourself.

MARY

to the priest.—Let you drink it up, holy father. Let you
drink it up, I'm saying, and not be letting on you wouldn't
do the like of it, and you with a stack of pint bottles above,
reaching the sky.

PRIEST

with resignation.—Well, here's to your good health, and God forgive us all.

[He drinks.

MARY

That's right now, your reverence, and the blessing of God be on you. Isn't it a grand thing to see you sitting down, with no pride in you, and drinking a sup with the like of us, and we the poorest, wretched, starving creatures you'd see any place on the earth?

PRIEST

If it's starving you are itself, I'm thinking it's well for the like of you that do be drinking when there's drouth on you, and lying down to sleep when your legs are stiff. (He sighs gloomily.) What would you do if it was the like of myself you were, saying Mass with your mouth dry, and running east and west for a sick call maybe, and hearing the rural people again and they saying their sins?

MARY

with compassion.—It's destroyed you must be hearing the sins of the rural people on a fine spring.

PRIEST

with despondency.—It's a hard life, I'm telling you, a hard life, Mary Byrne; and there's the bishop coming in the morning, and he an old man, would have you destroyed if he seen a thing at all.

MARY

with great sympathy.—It'd break my heart to hear you talking and sighing the like of that, your reverence. (She pats him on the knee.) Let you rouse up, now, if it's a poor, single man you are itself, and I'll be singing you songs unto the dawn of day.

PRIEST

interrupting her.—What is it I want with your songs when it'd be better for the like of you, that'll soon die, to be down on your two knees saying prayers to the Almighty God?

MARY

If it's prayers I want, you'd have a right to say one yourself, holy father; for we don't have them at all, and I've heard tell a power of times it's that you're for. Say one now, your reverence, for I've heard a power of queer things and I walking the world, but there's one thing I never heard any time, and that's a real priest saying a prayer.

PRIEST

The Lord protect us!

MARY

It's no lie, holy father. I often heard the rural people making a queer noise and they going to rest; but who'd mind the like of them? And I'm thinking it should be great game to hear a scholar, the like of you, speaking Latin to the saints above.

PRIEST

scandalized.—Stop your talking, Mary Byrne; you're an old flagrant heathen, and I'll stay no more with the lot of you.

[He rises.

MARY

catching hold of him.—Stop till you say a prayer, your reverence; stop till you say a little prayer, I'm telling you, and I'll give you my blessing and the last sup from the jug.

PRIEST

breaking away.—Leave me go, Mary Byrne; for I have never met your like for hard abominations the score and two years I'm living in the place.

MARY

innocently.—Is that the truth?

PRIEST

—It is, then, and God have mercy on your soul.

[The priest goes towards the left, and Sarah follows him.

SARAH

in a low voice.—And what time will you do the thing I'm asking, holy father? for I'm thinking you'll do it surely, and not have me growing into an old wicked heathen like herself.

MARY

calling out shrilly.—Let you be walking back here, Sarah Casey, and not be talking whisper-talk with the like of him in the face of the Almighty God.

SARAH

to the priest.—Do you hear her now, your reverence? Isn't it true, surely, she's an old, flagrant heathen, would destroy the world?

PRIEST

to Sarah, moving off.—Well, I'll be coming down early to the chapel, and let you come to me a while after you see me passing, and bring the bit of gold along with you, and the tin can. I'll marry you for them two, though it's a pitiful small sum; for I wouldn't be easy in my soul if I left you growing into an old, wicked heathen the like of her.

SARAH

following him out.—The blessing of the Almighty God be on you, holy father, and that He may reward and watch you from this present day.

MARY

nudging Michael.—Did you see that, Michael Byrne? Didn't you hear me telling you she's flighty a while back since the change of the moon? With her fussing for marriage, and she making whisper-talk with one man or another man along by the road.

MICHAEL

—Whist now, or she'll knock the head of you the time she comes back.

MARY

—Ah, it's a bad, wicked way the world is this night, if there's a fine air in it itself. You'd never have seen me, and I a young woman, making whisper-talk with the like of him, and he the fearfullest old fellow you'd see any place walking the world.

[Sarah comes back quickly.

MARY

calling out to her.—What is it you're after whispering above with himself?

SARAH

exultingly.—Lie down, and leave us in peace. She whispers with Michael.

MARY

poking out her pipe with a straw, sings—

She'd whisper with one, and she'd whisper with two—

She breaks off coughing.—My singing voice is gone for this night, Sarah Casey. (She lights her pipe.) But if it's flighty you are itself, you're a grand handsome woman, the glory of tinkers, the pride of Wicklow, the Beauty of Ballinacree. I wouldn't have you lying down and you lonesome to sleep this night in a dark ditch when the spring is coming in the trees; so let you sit down there by the big bough, and I'll be telling you the finest story you'd hear any place from Dundalk to Ballinacree, with great queens in it, making themselves matches from the start to the end, and they with shiny silks on them the length of the day, and white shifts for the night.

MICHAEL

standing up with the tin can in his hand.—Let you go asleep, and not have us destroyed.

MARY

lying back sleepily.—Don't mind him, Sarah Casey. Sit down now, and I'll be telling you a story would be fit to tell a woman the like of you in the springtime of the year.

SARAH

taking the can from Michael, and tying it up in a piece of sacking.—That'll not be rusting now in the dews of night. I'll put it up in the ditch the way it will be handy in the morning; and now we've that done, Michael Byrne, I'll go along with you and welcome for Tim Flaherty's hens.

[She puts the can in the ditch.

MARY

sleepily.—I've a grand story of the great queens of Ireland with white necks on them the like of Sarah Casey, and fine arms would hit you a slap the way Sarah Casey would hit you.

SARAH

beckoning on the left.—Come along now, Michael, while she's falling asleep.

[He goes towards left. Mary sees that they are going, starts up suddenly, and turns over on her hands and knees.

MARY

piteously.—Where is it you're going? Let you walk back here, and not be leaving me lonesome when the night is fine.

SARAH

Don't be waking the world with your talk when we're going up through the back wood to get two of Tim Flaherty's hens are roosting in the ash-tree above at the well.

MARY

And it's leaving me lone you are? Come back here, Sarah Casey. Come back here, I'm saying; or if it's off you must go, leave me the two little coppers you have, the way I can walk up in a short while, and get another pint for my sleep.

SARAH

It's too much you have taken. Let you stretch yourself out and take a long sleep; for isn't that the best thing any woman can do, and she an old drinking heathen like yourself.

[She and Michael go out left.

MARY

standing up slowly.—It's gone they are, and I with my feet that weak under me you'd knock me down with a rush, and my head with a noise in it the like of what you'd hear in a stream and it running between two rocks and rain falling. (She goes over to the ditch where the can is tied in sacking, and takes it down.) What good am I this night, God help me? What good are the grand stories I have when it's few would listen to an old woman, few but a girl maybe would be in great fear the time her hour was come, or a little child wouldn't be sleeping with the hunger on a cold night? (She takes the can from the sacking and fits in three empty bottles and straw in its place, and ties them up.) Maybe the two of them have a good right to be walking out the little short while they'd be young; but if they have itself, they'll not keep Mary Byrne from her full pint when the night's fine, and there's a dry moon in the sky. (She takes up the can, and puts the package back in the ditch.) Jemmy Neill's a decent lad; and he'll give me a good drop for the can; and maybe if I keep near the peelers to-morrow for the first bit of the fair, herself won't strike me at all; and if she does itself, what's a little stroke on your head beside sitting lonesome on a fine night, hearing the dogs barking, and the bats squeaking, and you saying over, it's a short while only till you die.

[She goes out singing "The night before Larry was stretched."

CURTAIN

ACT II.

SCENE: The same. Early morning. Sarah is washing her face in an old bucket; then plaits her hair. Michael is tidying himself also. Mary Byrne is asleep against the ditch.

SARAH

to Michael, with pleased excitement.—Go over, now, to the bundle beyond, and you'll find a kind of a red handkerchief to put upon your neck, and a green one for myself.

MICHAEL

getting them.—You're after spending more money on the like of them. Well, it's a power we're losing this time, and we not gaining a thing at all. (With the handkerchief.) Is it them two?

SARAH

It is, Michael. (She takes one of them.) Let you tackle that one round under your chin; and let you not forget to take your hat from your head when we go up into the church. I asked Biddy Flynn below, that's after marrying her second man, and she told me it's the like of that they do.

[Mary yawns, and turns over in her sleep.

SARAH

with anxiety.—There she is waking up on us, and I thinking we'd have the job done before she'd know of it at all.

MICHAEL

She'll be crying out now, and making game of us, and saying it's fools we are surely.

SARAH

I'll send her to sleep again, or get her out of it one way or another; for it'd be a bad case to have a divil's scholar the like of her turning the priest against us maybe with her godless talk.

MARY

waking up, and looking at them with curiosity, blandly.—That's fine things you have on you, Sarah Casey; and it's a great stir you're making this day, washing your face. I'm that used to the hammer, I wouldn't hear it at all, but washing is a rare thing, and you're after waking me up, and I having a great sleep in the sun.

[She looks around cautiously at the bundle in which she has hidden the bottles.

SARAH

coaxingly.—Let you stretch out again for a sleep, Mary Byrne, for it'll be a middling time yet before we go to the fair.

MARY

with suspicion.—That's a sweet tongue you have, Sarah Casey; but if sleep's a grand thing, it's a grand thing to be waking up a day the like of this, when there's a warm sun in it, and a kind air, and you'll hear the cuckoos singing and crying out on the top of the hills.

SARAH

If it's that gay you are, you'd have a right to walk down and see would you get a few halfpence from the rich men do be driving early to the fair.

MARY

When rich men do be driving early, it's queer tempers they have, the Lord forgive them; the way it's little but bad words and swearing out you'd get from them all.

SARAH

losing her temper and breaking out fiercely.—Then if you'll neither beg nor sleep, let you walk off from this place where you're not wanted, and not have us waiting for you maybe at the turn of day.

MARY

rather uneasy, turning to Michael.—God help our spirits, Michael; there she is again rousing cranky from the break of dawn. Oh! isn't she a terror since the moon did change? (She gets up slowly.) And I'd best be going forward to sell the gallon can.

[She goes over and takes up the bundle.

SARAH

crying out angrily.—Leave that down, Mary Byrne. Oh! aren't you the scorn of women to think that you'd have that drouth and roguery on you that you'd go drinking the can and the dew not dried from the grass?

MARY

in a feigned tone of pacification, with the bundle still in her hand.—It's not a drouth but a heartburn I have this day, Sarah Casey, so I'm going down to cool my gullet at the blessed well; and I'll sell the can to the parson's daughter below, a harmless poor creature would fill your hand with shillings for a brace of lies.

SARAH

Leave down the tin can, Mary Byrne, for I hear the drouth upon your tongue to-day.

MARY

There's not a drink-house from this place to the fair, Sarah Casey; the way you'll find me below with the full price, and not a farthing gone.

[She turns to go off left.

SARAH

jumping up, and picking up the hammer threateningly.—Put down that can, I'm saying.

MARY

looking at her for a moment in terror, and putting down the bundle in the ditch.—Is it raving mad you're going, Sarah Casey, and you the pride of women to destroy the world?

SARAH

going up to her, and giving her a push off left.—I'll show you if it's raving mad I am. Go on from this place, I'm saying, and be wary now.

MARY

turning back after her.—If I go, I'll be telling old and young you're a weathered heathen savage, Sarah Casey, the one did put down a head of the parson's cabbage to boil in the pot with your clothes (the Priest comes in behind her, on the left, and listens), and quenched the flaming candles on the throne of God the time your shadow fell within the pillars of the chapel door.

[Sarah turns on her, and she springs round nearly into the Priest's arms. When she sees him, she claps her shawl over her mouth, and goes up towards the ditch, laughing to herself.

PRIEST

going to Sarah, half terrified at the language that he has heard.—Well, aren't you a fearful lot? I'm thinking it's only humbug you were making at the fall of night, and you won't need me at all.

SARAH

with anger still in her voice.—Humbug is it! Would you be turning back upon your spoken promise in the face of God?

PRIEST

dubiously.—I'm thinking you were never christened, Sarah

Casey; and it would be a queer job to go dealing Christian sacraments unto the like of you. (Persuasively feeling in his pocket.) So it would be best, maybe, I'd give you a shilling for to drink my health, and let you walk on, and not trouble me at all.

SARAH

That's your talking, is it? If you don't stand to your spoken word, holy father, I'll make my own complaint to the mitred bishop in the face of all.

PRIEST

You'd do that!

SARAH

I would surely, holy father, if I walked to the city of Dublin with blood and blisters on my naked feet.

PRIEST

uneasily scratching his ear.—I wish this day was done, Sarah Casey; for I'm thinking it's a risky thing getting mixed up in any matters with the like of you.

SARAH

Be hasty then, and you'll have us done with before you'd think at all.

PRIEST

giving in.—Well, maybe it's right you are, and let you come up to the chapel when you see me looking from the door.

[He goes up into the chapel.

SARAH

calling after him.—We will, and God preserve you, holy father.

MARY

coming down to them, speaking with amazement and consternation, but without anger.—Going to the chapel! It's at marriage you're fooling again, maybe? (Sarah turns her back on her.) It was for that you were washing your face, and you after sending me for porter at the fall of night the way I'd drink a good half from the jug? (Going round in front of Sarah.) Is it at marriage you're fooling again?

SARAH

triumphantly.—It is, Mary Byrne. I'll be married now in a short while; and from this day there will no one have a right to call me a dirty name and I selling cans in Wicklow or Wexford or the city of Dublin itself.

MARY

turning to Michael.—And it's yourself is wedding her, Michael Byrne?

MICHAEL

gloomily.—It is, God spare us.

MARY

looks at Sarah for a moment, and then bursts out into a laugh of derision.—Well, she's a tight, hardy girl, and it's no lie; but I never knew till this day it was a black born fool I had for a son. You'll breed asses, I've heard them say, and poaching dogs, and horses'd go licking the wind, but it's a hard thing, God help me, to breed sense in a son.

MICHAEL

gloomily.—If I didn't marry her, she'd be walking off to Jaunting Jim maybe at the fall of night; and it's well yourself knows there isn't the like of her for getting money and selling songs to the men.

MARY

And you're thinking it's paying gold to his reverence would make a woman stop when she's a mind to go?

SARAH

angrily.—Let you not be destroying us with your talk when I've as good a right to a decent marriage as any speckled female does be sleeping in the black hovels above, would choke a mule.

MARY

soothingly.—It's as good a right you have surely, Sarah Casey, but what good will it do? Is it putting that ring on your finger will keep you from getting an aged woman and losing the fine face you have, or be easing your pains, when it's the grand ladies do be married in silk dresses, with rings of gold, that do pass any woman with their share of torment in the hour of birth, and do be paying the doctors in the city of Dublin a great price at that time, the like of what you'd pay for a good ass and a cart?

[She sits down.

SARAH

puzzled.—Is that the truth?

MARY

pleased with the point she has made.—Wouldn't any know it's the truth? Ah, it's a few short years you are yet in the world, Sarah Casey, and it's little or nothing at all maybe you know about it.

SARAH

vehement but uneasy.—What is it yourself knows of the fine ladies when they wouldn't let the like of you go near them at all?

MARY

If you do be drinking a little sup in one town and another town, it's soon you get great knowledge and a great sight into the world. You'll see men there, and women there, sitting up on the ends of barrels in the dark night, and they making great talk would soon have the like of you, Sarah Casey, as wise as a March hare.

MICHAEL

to Sarah.—That's the truth she's saying, and maybe if you've sense in you at all, you'd have a right still to leave your fooling, and not be wasting our gold.

SARAH

decisively.—If it's wise or fool I am, I've made a good bargain and I'll stand to it now.

MARY

What is it he's making you give?

MICHAEL

The ten shillings in gold, and the tin can is above tied in the sack.

MARY

looking at the bundle with surprise and dread.—The bit of gold and the tin can, is it?

MICHAEL

The half a sovereign, and the gallon can.

MARY

scrambling to her feet quickly.—Well, I think I'll be walking off the road to the fair the way you won't be destroying me going too fast on the hills. (She goes a few steps towards the left, then turns and speaks to Sarah very persuasively.) Let you not take the can from the sack, Sarah Casey; for the people is coming above would be making game of you, and pointing their fingers if they seen you do the like of that. Let you leave it safe in the bag, I'm saying, Sarah darling. It's that way will be best.

[She goes towards left, and pauses for a moment, looking about her with embarrassment.

MICHAEL

in a low voice.—What ails her at all?

SARAH

anxiously.—It's real wicked she does be when you hear her speaking as easy as that.

MARY

to herself.—I'd be safer in the chapel, I'm thinking; for if she caught me after on the road, maybe she would kill me then.

[She comes hobbling back towards the right.

SARAH

Where is it you're going? It isn't that way we'll be walking to the fair.

MARY

I'm going up into the chapel to give you my blessing and hear the priest saying his prayers. It's a lonesome road is running below to Greenane, and a woman would never know the things might happen her and she walking single in a lonesome place.

[As she reaches the chapel-gate, the Priest comes to it in his surplice.

PRIEST

crying out.—Come along now. It is the whole day you'd keep me here saying my prayers, and I getting my death with not a bit in my stomach, and my breakfast in ruins, and the Lord Bishop maybe driving on the road to-day?

SARAH

We're coming now, holy father.

PRIEST

Give me the bit of gold into my hand.

SARAH

It's here, holy father.

[She gives it to him. Michael takes the bundle from the ditch and brings it over, standing a little behind Sarah. He feels the bundle, and looks at Mary with a meaning look.

PRIEST

looking at the gold.—It's a good one, I'm thinking, wherever you got it. And where is the can?

SARAH

taking the bundle.—We have it here in a bit of clean sack, your reverence. We tied it up in the inside of that to keep it from rusting in the dews of night, and let you not open it now or you'll have the people making game of us and telling the story on us, east and west to the butt of the hills.

PRIEST

taking the bundle.—Give it here into my hand, Sarah Casey. What is it any person would think of a tinker making a can.

[He begins opening the bundle.

SARAH

It's a fine can, your reverence. for if it's poor simple people we are, it's fine cans we can make, and himself, God help him, is a great man surely at the trade.

[Priest opens the bundle; the three empty bottles fall out.

SARAH

Glory to the saints of joy!

PRIEST

Did ever any man see the like of that? To think you'd be putting deceit on me, and telling lies to me, and I going to marry you for a little sum wouldn't marry a child.

SARAH

crestfallen and astonished.—It's the divil did it, your reverence, and I wouldn't tell you a lie. (Raising her hands.) May the Lord Almighty strike me dead if the divil isn't after hooshing the tin can from the bag.

PRIEST

vehemently.—Go along now, and don't be swearing your lies. Go along now, and let you not be thinking I'm big fool enough to believe the like of that, when it's after selling it you are or making a swap for drink of it, maybe, in the darkness of the night.

MARY

in a peacemaking voice, putting her hand on the Priest's left arm.—She wouldn't do the like of that, your reverence, when she hasn't a decent standing drouth on her at all; and she's setting great store on her marriage the way you'd have a right to be taking her easy, and not minding the can. What differ would an empty can make with a fine, rich, hardy man the like of you?

SARAH

imploringly.—Marry us, your reverence, for the ten shillings in gold, and we'll make you a grand can in the evening—a can would be fit to carry water for the holy man of God. Marry us now and I'll be saying fine prayers for you, morning and night, if it'd be raining itself, and it'd be in two black pools I'd be setting my knees.

PRIEST

loudly.—It's a wicked, thieving, lying, scheming lot you are, the pack of you. Let you walk off now and take every stinking rag you have there from the ditch.

MARY

putting her shawl over her head.—Marry her, your reverence, for the love of God, for there'll be queer doings below if you send her off the like of that and she swearing crazy on the road.

SARAH

angrily.—It's the truth she's saying; for it's herself, I'm thinking, is after swapping the tin can for a pint, the time she was raging mad with the drouth, and ourselves above walking the hill.

MARY

crying out with indignation.—Have you no shame, Sarah Casey, to tell lies unto a holy man?

SARAH

to Mary, working herself into a rage.—It's making game of me you'd be, and putting a fool's head on me in the face of the world; but if you were thinking to be mighty cute walking off, or going up to hide in the church, I've got you this time, and you'll not run from me now.

She seizes up one of the bottles.

MARY

hiding behind the priest.—Keep her off, your reverence, keep her off for the love of the Almighty God. What at all would the Lord Bishop say if he found me here lying with my head broken across, or the two of yous maybe digging a bloody grave for me at the door of the church?

PRIEST

waving Sarah off.—Go along, Sarah Casey. Would you be doing murder at my feet? Go along from me now, and wasn't I a big fool to have to do with you when it's nothing but distraction and torment I get from the kindness of my heart?

SARAH

shouting.—I've bet a power of strong lads east and west through the world, and are you thinking I'd turn back from a priest? Leave the road now, or maybe I would strike yourself.

PRIEST

You would not, Sarah Casey. I've no fear for the lot of you; but let you walk off, I'm saying, and not be coming where you've no business, and screeching tumult and murder at the doorway of the church.

SARAH

I'll not go a step till I have her head broke, or till I'm wed with himself. If you want to get shut of us, let you marry us now, for I'm thinking the ten shillings in gold is a good price for the like of you, and you near burst with the fat.

PRIEST

I wouldn't have you coming in on me and soiling my church; for there's nothing at all, I'm thinking, would keep the like of you from hell. (He throws down the ten shillings on the ground.) Gather up your gold now, and begone from my sight, for if ever I set an eye on you again you'll hear me telling the peelers who it was stole the black ass belonging to Philly O'Cullen, and whose hay it is the grey ass does be eating.

SARAH

You'd do that?

PRIEST

I would, surely.

SARAH

If you do, you'll be getting all the tinkers from Wicklow and Wexford, and the County Meath, to put up block tin in the place of glass to shield your windows where you do be looking out and blinking at the girls. It's hard set you'll be that time, I'm telling you, to fill the depth of your belly the long days of Lent; for we wouldn't leave a laying pullet in your yard at all.

PRIEST

losing his temper finally.—Go on, now, or I'll send the Lords of Justice a dated story of your villainies—burning, stealing, robbing, raping to this mortal day. Go on now, I'm saying, if you'd run from Kilmainham or the rope itself.

MICHAEL

taking off his coat.—Is it run from the like of you, holy father? Go up to your own shanty, or I'll beat you with the ass's reins till the world would hear you roaring from this place to the coast of Clare.

PRIEST

Is it lift your hand upon myself when the Lord would blight your members if you'd touch me now? Go on from this.

[He gives him a shove.

MICHAEL

Blight me is it? Take it then, your reverence, and God help you so.

[He runs at him with the reins.

PRIEST

runs up to ditch crying out.—There are the peelers passing by the grace of God—hey, below!

MARY

clapping her hand over his mouth.—Knock him down on the road; they didn't hear him at all.

[Michael pulls him down.

SARAH

Gag his jaws.

MARY

Stuff the sacking in his teeth.

[They gag him with the sack that had the can in it.

SARAH

Tie the bag around his head, and if the peelers come, we'll put him head-first in the boghole is beyond the ditch.

[They tie him up in some sacking.

MICHAEL

to Mary.—Keep him quiet, and the rags tight on him for fear he'd screech. (He goes back to their camp.) Hurry with the things, Sarah Casey. The peelers aren't coming this way, and maybe we'll get off from them now.

[They bundle the things together in wild haste, the priest wriggling and struggling about on the ground, with old Mary trying to keep him quiet.

MARY

patting his head.—Be quiet, your reverence. What is it ails you, with your wrigglings now? Is it choking maybe? (She puts her hand under the sack, and feels his mouth, patting him on the back.) It's only letting on you are, holy father, for your nose is blowing back and forward as easy as an east wind on an April day. (In a soothing voice.) There now, holy father, let you stay easy, I'm telling you, and learn a little sense and patience, the way you'll not be so airy again going to rob poor sinners of their scraps of gold. (He gets quieter.) That's a good boy you are now, your reverence, and let you not be uneasy, for we wouldn't hurt you at all. It's sick and sorry we are to tease you; but what did you want meddling with the like of us, when it's a long time we are going our own ways—father and son, and his son after him, or mother and daughter, and her own daughter again—and it's little need we ever had of going up into a church and swearing—I'm told there's swearing with it—a word no man would believe, or with drawing rings on our fingers, would be cutting our skins maybe when we'd be taking the ass from the shafts, and pulling the straps the time they'd be slippy with going around beneath the heavens in rains falling.

MICHAEL

who has finished bundling up the things, comes over to Sarah.—We're fixed now; and I have a mind to run him in a boghole the way he'll not be tattling to the peelers of our games to-day.

SARAH

You'd have a right too, I'm thinking.

MARY

soothingly.—Let you not be rough with him, Sarah Casey, and he after drinking his sup of porter with us at the fall of night. Maybe he'd swear a mighty oath he wouldn't harm us, and then we'd safer loose him; for if we went to drown him, they'd maybe hang the batch of us, man and child and woman, and the ass itself.

MICHAEL

What would he care for an oath?

MARY

Don't you know his like do live in terror of the wrath of God? (Putting her mouth to the Priest's ear in the sacking.) Would you swear an oath, holy father, to leave us in our freedom, and not talk at all? (Priest nods in sacking.) Didn't I tell you? Look at the poor fellow nodding his head off in the bias of the sacks. Strip them off from him, and he'll be easy now.

MICHAEL

as if speaking to a horse.—Hold up, holy father.

[He pulls the sacking off, and shows the priest with his hair on end. They free his mouth.

MARY

Hold him till he swears.

PRIEST

in a faint voice.—I swear surely. If you let me go in peace, I'll not inform against you or say a thing at all, and may God forgive me for giving heed unto your like to-day.

SARAH

puts the ring on his finger.—There's the ring, holy father, to keep you minding of your oath until the end of time; for my heart's scalded with your fooling; and it'll be a long day till I go making talk of marriage or the like of that.

MARY

complacently, standing up slowly.—She's vexed now, your reverence; and let you not mind her at all, for she's right surely, and it's little need we ever had of the like of you to get us our bit to eat, and our bit to drink, and our time of love when we were young men and women, and were fine to look at.

MICHAEL

Hurry on now. He's a great man to have kept us from fooling our gold; and we'll have a great time drinking that bit with the trampers on the green of Clash.

[They gather up their things. The priest stands up.

PRIEST

lifting up his hand.—I've sworn not to call the hand of man upon your crimes to-day; but I haven't sworn I wouldn't call the fire of heaven from the hand of the Almighty God.

[He begins saying a Latin malediction in a loud ecclesiastical voice.

MARY

There's an old villain.

ALL

together.—Run, run. Run for your lives.

[They rush out, leaving the Priest master of the situation.

CURTAIN

Scribbling Notes

CHAPTER XXII

People will always need people

People will always need people

by Benjamin Zephaniah
    People need people,
To walk to
To talk to
To cry and rely on,
People will always need people.
To love and to miss
To hug and to kiss,
It's useful to have other people.
To whom to moan
If you're all alone,
It's so hard to share
When no one is there.
There's not much to do
When there's no one but you.
People will always need people.
    To please
To tease
To put you at ease,
People will always need people.
To make life appealing
And give life some meaning,
It's useful to have other people.
It you need a change
To whom will you turn.

If you need a lesson
From whom will you learn.
If you need to play
You'll know why I say
People will always need people.
    As girlfriends
As boyfriends
From Bombay
To Ostend,
People will always need people-
To have friendly fights with
And share tasty bites with,
It's useful to have other people.
People live in families
Gangs, posses and packs,
Its seems we need company
Before we relax,
So stop making enemies
And let's face the facts,
People will always need people,
Yes
People will always need people.
    Scribbling Notes

CHAPTER XXIII

Faith Healing BY PHILIP LARKIN

Faith Healing

BY PHILIP LARKIN

Slowly the women file to where he stands
Upright in rimless glasses, silver hair,
Dark suit, white collar. Stewards tirelessly
Persuade them onwards to his voice and hands,
Within whose warm spring rain of loving care
Each dwells some twenty seconds. Now, dear child,
What's wrong, the deep American voice demands,
And, scarcely pausing, goes into a prayer
Directing God about this eye, that knee.
Their heads are clasped abruptly; then, exiled
Like losing thoughts, they go in silence; some
Sheepishly stray, not back into their lives
Just yet; but some stay stiff, twitching and loud
With deep hoarse tears, as if a kind of dumb
And idiot child within them still survives
To re-awake at kindness, thinking a voice
At last calls them alone, that hands have come
To lift and lighten; and such joy arrives
Their thick tongues blort, their eyes squeeze grief, a crowd
Of huge unheard answers jam and rejoice—
What's wrong! Moustached in flowered frocks they shake:
By now, all's wrong. In everyone there sleeps

A sense of life lived according to love.
To some it means the difference they could make
By loving others, but across most it sweeps
As all they might have done had they been loved.
That nothing cures. An immense slackening ache,
As when, thawing, the rigid landscape weeps,
Spreads slowly through them—that, and the voice above
Saying Dear child, and all time has disproved.

Philip Larkin, "Faith Healing" from Whitsun Weddings. Copyright © Estate of Philip Larkin. Reprinted by permission of Faber and Faber, Ltd.

Source: Collected Poems (Farrar Straus and Giroux, 2001)

Scribbling Notes